Type 2 Diabetes Crock Pot Cookbook

Affordable, Easy and Healthy Budget Friendly Recipes to Prevent and Reverse Type 2 Diabetes

By Olivia Steven

Copyrights©2019 By Olivia Steven
All Rights Reserved

This document is geared towards providing exact and reliable information in regards to the topic and issue covered. The publication is sold with the idea that the publisher is not required to render accounting, officially permitted, or otherwise, qualified services. If advice is necessary, legal or professional, a practiced individual in the profession should be ordered.

Legal Notice: The book is copyright protected. This is only for personal use. You cannot amend, distribute, sell, use, quote or paraphrase any part or the content within this book without the consent of the author.

Under no circumstance will any legal responsibility or blame be held against the publisher for any reparation, damages, or monetary loss due to the information herein, either directly or indirectly.

Disclaimer Notice: Please note the information contained within this document is for educational and entertainment purpose only. Every attempt has been made to provide accurate, up to date and reliable complete information. No warranties of any kind are expressed or implied. Reader acknowledge that the author is not engaging in the rendering of legal, financial, medical or professional advice. The content of this book has been derived from various sources. Please consult a licensed professional before attempting any techniques outlined in this book.

Table of Content

Introduction 1

Chapter 1: Diabetes 101 2
   What is Diabetes? 3
   Turning Diabetes Around 4
   Packing Power Into Every Meal 6
   Complete Nutrition For Diabetics 9

Chapter 2: Crockpot 101 11
   What is Crockpot? 11
   The Features And Functions of a Crock pot 13
   Tips For a Better Experience With a Crockpot 14

Chapter 3: 21 Day Diabetic Meal Plan 15

Chapter 4 Breakfast And Brunch 19
   Dreamy Lemon Berry Steel Cut Oats 19
   Mouth-Watering Egg Casserole 20
   Wonderful Spicy Breakfast Casserole 21
   Amazing Overnight Apple and Cinnamon Oatmeal 22
   Apple Cinnamon Oatmeal 23
   Breakfast Casserole 24
   Cauliflower Oatmeal 25
   Crockpot Breakfast Casserole 26

Chapter 5 Vegan And Vegetable 28
   Vegetable Soup 28
   Almond Toffee Topped Pears 29
   Hearty Cabbage Soup 30
   Vegan Thai Mushroom Soup 31

Individual Egg and Vegetable Frittatas...32

Chicken Curry Salad..33

Asian Spaghetti Squash...34

Easy Black Bean Soup...35

Chapter 6 Fish And Seafood 37

Tilapia Stew with Green Peppers...37

Succulent Salmon with Caramelized Onions...38

Seafood Gumbo Stock..39

Simple Poached Salmon...40

Sophia Homemade Crockpot Seafood Stock...41

10-minute Crockpot Salmon..42

Lemon Pepper Salmon...43

Simple Steamed Crab Legs..44

Chapter 7 Poultry...46

Chicken Noodle Soup...46

Chicken Mushroom Stew...47

Tomato Balsamic Crockpot Chicken...48

Turkey in Cream Sauce..49

Slow Simmered Crockpot Chicken with Raisins, Capers and Basil......................50

Turkey Breast with Gravy..51

Caribbean Curried Chicken..52

Turkey with Berry Compote..53

Chapter 8 Beef Lamb And Pork...55

Slow-cooked Flank Steak...55

Sassy Pot Roast..56

Shredded Green Chili Beef..57

Pork Stew...58

Mexican Meatloaf..59

Chipotle Steak Simmer..60

    Flank Steak Tacos.. 61

    Pork and Pumpkin Stew.. 62

Chapter 9 Soups Stews And Curries... **64**

    Rutabaga Stew... 64

    Coconut Shrimp Curry Recipe.. 65

    Split Pea Soup... 66

    Easter Ham Bone Soup... 67

    Pork And Green Chile Stew.. 68

    Beefed-Up Vegetable Stew... 69

    Flemish Beef Stew.. 70

    French Onion Soup... 71

Chapter 10 Snacks... **73**

    Scotch Eggs.. 73

    No Peel Crockpot Hard-Boiled Eggs... 74

    Deviled Eggs.. 75

    Turkey Breasts... 76

    Pumpkin Muffins.. 77

    Popcorns... 78

    Meatloaf on A Sling... 79

    Chipotle BBQ Pork Folded Tacos.. 80

Chapter 11 Desserts... **82**

    Creme Brulee.. 82

    Cider Applesauce... 83

    Crockpot Sugar-Free Chocolate Molten Lava Cake... 84

    Maple Custard.. 85

    Fudge Cake... 86

    Key Lime Dump Cake.. 87

    Peppermint Chocolate Pudding Cake... 88

Introduction

I strongly believe that everyone's journey with diabetes is different. However, even with all the complications of diabetes, nothing should stop you from enjoying life or doing the things that you love. That's the way it should be!

I have mentioned several times in my cookbooks that, as a registered dietitian, I hate seeing people get enslaved by their dietary habits. Diabetes is a chronic condition that, over the last couple of years, has become widespread. One thing that is driving the proliferation of diabetes cases is our lifestyle and the changing dietary habits.

We've become so busy in our work life that we don't have time to prepare nice, healthy meals at home. As a result, we depend largely on fast foods, and this is where the rain started beating us.

Because of our poor dietary habits, we are at crossroads with our health, and conditions like diabetes are now a permanent fixture.

But that's not what worries me most. What worries me is the community that has gone all out to make healthy eating difficult for people of all walks. Besides, I'm always gutted when I dive online, only to find a sea of dieting information and plenty of fads that misled and trap many in poor eating habits.

I sat down and thought, how can we save people from the jaws of the confusing web of food? The option was to create a cookbook with easy to cook, delicious, and completely versatile meals. This cookbook will give you all the information you need to know about diabetes from Type 1 and Type 2 diabetes to gestational diabetes. Most importantly, I will introduce you to one of the fascinating cooking appliances: the crockpot.

Additionally, you will find easy recipes to keep on the path to a healthier, fun, and long life with diabetes. Moreover, I have prepared a 21 days meal plan to kick start your life with diabetes. The plan will help you eat healthier without breaking the bank. I choose 5 ingredients or less meals to make cooking easy for everyone.

Whether you have diabetes or have a friend or family with diabetes, this cookbook has the information you need to make life with diabetes sustainable. I am pretty sure that you won't get bored, and you'll scale above the hurdles of diabetes to enjoy your life. This is the key to a happy and satisfying life with diabetes.

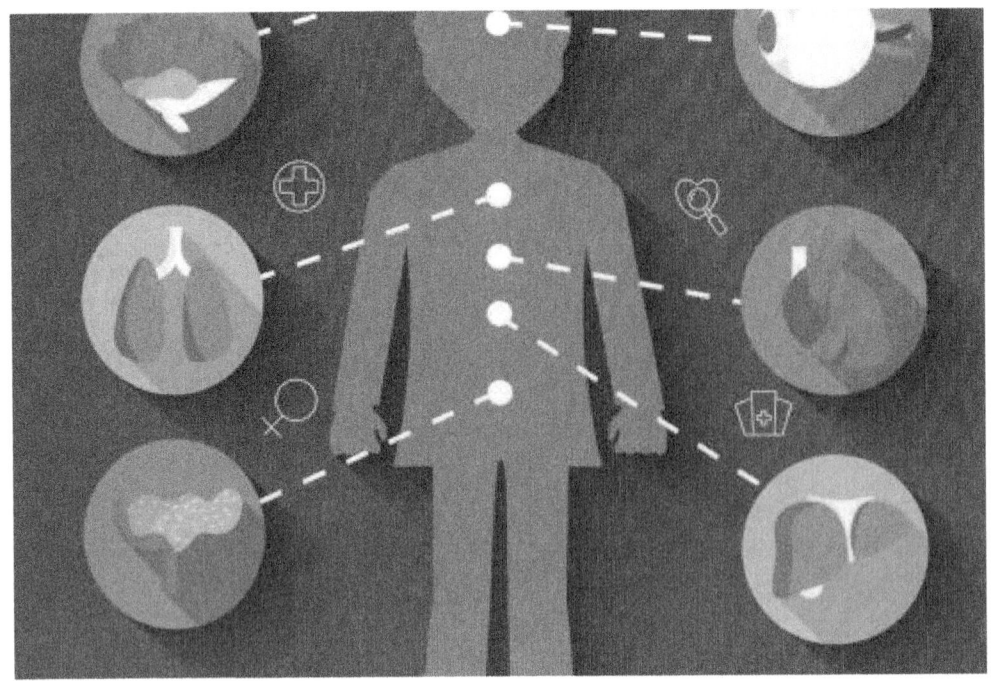

Chapter 1: Diabetes 101

According to the American Diabetes Association, 30.3 million Us citizens or 9.4% of the population had diabetes in 2015. Needless to say, this number is getting even bigger as the days go by. This is a worrying stat, but its reality we all are grappling with.

Now, if you aren't amongst the 30.3 million people with diabetes, you probably have a close relative or friend with it. This means if we are to deal with this rampaging menace, we have to join hands and deliver the telling impact of our collective efforts.

However, keeping diabetes under control is not a cakewalk, especially when you consider the modern eating habits. But we can't let our own eating habits drive us into the grave. As a result, we have to keep fighting until the diabetes menace shows us its back. But, as you know, to solve any problem you must get to the bottom of it and understand its root cause.

It's because of this reason that I have written this introductory chapter to introduce you to diabetes.

Let's roll!

What is Diabetes?

Diabetes mellitus or simply diabetes is a widespread health condition where the blood sugar is too high. Actually, diabetes is a cluster of health conditions that inhibits the production of insulin or cause insulin not to work properly or a combination of the two. When either or both of these insulin complications strike, they cause the blood sugar to accumulate to harmful levels, hence diabetes.

To understand diabetes better, you first have to understand how insulin is produced and used in the body. Insulin is produced in the pancreas by cells known as the islet of Langerhans, which are spread throughout the pancreas. 75% of these cells make insulin whereas, 20% produce glucagon.

Insulin is tasked with maintaining the blood glucose within the healthy levels. On the other hand, glucagon raises blood sugar level. From this, you can see the function of the pancreas cell is counterproductive when it comes to controlling diabetes.

What happens is, when food is metabolized normally, the pancreas releases insulin to counteract the rising blood glucose levels. When insulin levels fall, less glucose is stored in the form of glycogen, hence the build-up.

The cases of diabetes have proliferated in recent times, impelled by unhealthy eating habits. This doesn't mean the diabetes is entirely new; actually, the chronic condition has been around since 100 AD. The term diabetes was coined from the Greek word for "flow-through." Primarily, the condition was described by its two core symptoms urinating frequently and extreme thirst.

Turning Diabetes Around

There are three types of diabetes you need to know. They include:

Type 1 Diabetes

Initially, the type one diabetes was known as insulin-dependent diabetes mellitus (IDDM). It's a condition where the pancreas makes hardly any insulin or no insulin at all. Unfortunately, the causes of type 1 diabetes remain unknown.

Health experts believe that type 1 diabetes is an autoimmune disease. This means that a condition causes the immune system to suppress the normal functioning or destroy the islet of Langerhans. As a result, the body is unable to produce enough insulin to regulate blood sugar.

Type 1 diabetes is widespread in young adults and children. This is the reason it was known by the term juvenile-onset diabetes. Generally, people with this type 1 diabetes have to inject insulin into their bodies to keep the condition under control.

Symptoms Of Type 1 Diabetes

- Frequent urination
- Increased thirst
- Fatigues and weakness
- Extreme hunger
- Mood changes such as irritability
- Unintended weight loss
- Blurred vision.

Foods For Type 1 Diabetes

Initially, health experts thought there was a special group of food for people with diabetes. They believed that people who have diabetes had to avoid certain foods like foods with sugar. However, that seemed not to be the case, especially for people with type 1 diabetes.

Indeed, people with type 1 diabetes can eat the same foods as everyone, provided that the meals are healthy. The only difference is that they have to cut the consumption of unhealthy fat and eat foods with plenty of fiber.

Type 2 Diabetes

Type 2 diabetes was commonly known as non-insulin-dependent diabetes mellitus (NIDDM). With type 2 diabetes, the pancreas produces insulin, but the amount is not enough to regulate blood sugar. In other cases, the pancreas produces insulin in large quantities, but the body, for some reason, cannot utilize it properly.

Unlike type 1 diabetes, type 2 diabetes is widespread in adults over 40 years old, hence the name of adult-onset diabetes. In most cases, type 2 diabetes is common in overweight people or those from a family with a history of diabetes.

Interestingly, 90% of diabetes cases are type 2 diabetes. Besides, 80% of type 2 diabetes patients are overweight. This is the reason why being overweight is seen as a trigger of type 2 diabetes. People with type 2 diabetes can control this condition with weight control. This means adopting proper dieting and a strict exercise regimen to achieve weight control.

Also, in most cases, people with type 2 diabetes do not need to inject insulin to manage their conditions. In some serious case, it takes the combination of weight control, oral medication, and insulin injection to control type 2 diabetes.

Symptoms Of Type 2 Diabetes

All type 1 diabetes symptoms are type 2 diabetes symptoms. Other symptoms include:

- Slow healing of wounds and cuts
- Numbness, tingling, or pain in feet and hands.
- Yeast infection and itching
- Patches of dark skin

Foods For Type 2 Diabetes

People with type 2 diabetes can take meals with varying ratios of protein, fats, and carbohydrates. The proteins and fats should primarily be obtained from plant sources. On the other hand, carbohydrates should come from low glycemic foods like vegetables.

Gestational

The third type of diabetes is known as gestational diabetes, which occurs during pregnancy. What happens is that during pregnancy, there are a lot of hormonal changes. Some of these changes may cause a build-up of blood glucose. In other cases, the demand for insulin rises, and the pancreas is unable to keep up with the demand.

One interesting fact is that nearly a third of women with gestational diabetes are highly likely to develop type 2 diabetes. Also, since it occurs during pregnancy, it's difficult to deal with it using oral medication. This is because oral drugs can affect the fetus. The best way to deal with gestational diabetes is proper dieting and exercise. In some serious cases, insulin injection is required to lower blood glucose.

The symptoms of gestational diabetes include unusual thirst, fatigue, frequent urination, and sugar in the urine. Luckily, these symptoms fade away when the baby is born.

Packing Power Into Every Meal

What you need to know is that diabetes has no cure. However, with the right care and attention, you can keep it under control. This means making unique lifestyle commitments, constantly monitoring blood sugar, and adopting proper exercise routine. Above all, you must curb the poor dietary habits and pack power into every meal you take.

As you may have noticed, medical nutrition therapy is of paramount importance when it comes to diabetes management. Unfortunately, there are a lot of misconceptions concerning diabetes and nutrition. In this chapter, we'll reveal the details you need to know about diabetes and the core nutrients.

Carbohydrates

Studies have shown that people with diabetes need to consume foods containing normal carbohydrates. In particular, people with diabetes should endeavor to eat carbs from fruits, whole grain, low-fat milk, and vegetables.

So, how many carbs should people with diabetes eat?

One thing you need to know is that there is no "one size fits all" carbs level for everyone. Why? Because our bodies are created to be different. Besides, there are other significant factors to put into consideration when deciding the carb count, including weight, gender, activity level, and age.

What we know is that people with diabetes should obtain 45% of their calories from carbohydrates. For example, women with diabetes need 3 - 4 servings per meal. On the other hand, men require 4-5 carbs servings per meal. One carb serving is equal to 15g per serving.

To be on the safe side, work with qualified medical professionals, and dietitians to establish the exact carb goal. You also need to constantly count carbs to maintain your blood sugar levels within a healthy range.

Proteins

Proteins help your body grow and are as vital as other macronutrients. Because of this, people with diabetes need to consume proteins. However, they need to understand what happens when you consume proteins.

As mentioned earlier, protein helps the body develop new tissues. But besides this, protein is broken into glucose, which is used for energy in the body. However, unlike carbohydrates, proteins are metabolized into glucose less efficiently. Consequently, the impact of protein on the level of glucose in the blood may take a few to several hours to occur.

People with diabetes need to take into account the effects of protein before taking protein-based meals. It's advisable that you understand how the sugar levels may react to such meals. This will help you know the exact insulin requirements for your body.

The recommended protein intake varies by age:
- 1-3 years: 15 grams
- 4-6 years: 20 grams
- 7-10 years: 28 grams
- 11-14 years: 42 grams
- 15-18 years: 55 grams
- 19-50 years: 55 grams
- Over 50 years: 53 grams

Dietary Fat

Fat, like carbohydrates, get a lot of attention when it comes to diabetes management. There is no doubt diabetics need to control their fat intake to curb the risk of developing heart disease. More crucial than the total fat is the type (healthy or unhealthy) of fat you consume. Not all fats are good for you, that's why it's important to learn the difference.

Unhealthy Fats

Unhealthy fats include saturated fats from foods like high-fat dairy products, high-fat meats, lard, butter, chocolate, cream sauces, and poultry skin. The goal should be to consume less than 10% of calories from these types of foods.

Other unhealthy fats include trans-fat and cholesterol. One thing to know about trans-fat is that they increase cholesterol levels in the blood. This type of fat is worse than saturated fat, and you should eat as less trans fats as you can. Trans fat is contained in processed foods, stick margarine, and fast foods. On the other hand, cholesterol is contained in high-fat meat, poultry skin, egg yolk, and high-fat dairy products.

Healthy Fats

Whether you have diabetes or not, you should eat the following healthy fats. One is monounsaturated fat, which is also known as healthy or good fats. This type of fat lowers bad (LDL) cholesterol. Foods that contain monounsaturated fats include canola oil, avocado, olive oil, nuts, peanut butter & oil, and sesame seeds.

Another type of healthy fat is polyunsaturated fat, which is obtained from plant-based oil, walnuts, salad dressings, sunflower oil, mayonnaise, and soft margarine. Besides, you should eat omega3 fatty acids from foods like herring, mackerel, albacore tuna, salmon, rainbow trout, and sardines.

Complete Nutrition For Diabetics

Now that you know the nutrients you need to manage diabetes, it's time to look into the healthy food groups for diabetes. Remember, the foods you consume makes a big difference in the way you manage diabetes. Besides, the foods contribute greatly to how well you feel and how much energy you gain.

There are four main food groups for people with diabetes. They include:

Vegetable and Fruits

Naturally, veggies and fruits pack a punch in terms of fiber, minerals, and vitamins. Not just that, fruits and veggies contain low calories, which is good for people with diabetes. In fact, living with diabetes should not stop you from eating fruits and vegetables.

You have them the way you want, dried, fresh, canned, or frozen. You should try to eat a variety of fruits to get as many minerals and vitamins as possible. However, try to avoid smoothies and juices; they offer no value in terms of fiber content.

One thing to note is that, as much as you try to limit the number of carbs you consume, you need to include fruits and veggies in your meals. Having them in your meal protects against heart disease, some types of cancers, stroke, and high blood pressure.

Starchy Foods

Starch is obtained from rice, potatoes, pasta, naan, chapattis, and plantain. These foods provided glucose, which is broken down in the body for energy. While glucose is needed to power the body cells, getting it in high quantities can be detrimental to the health of people with diabetes.

Some starchy foods can cause a sudden rise in blood glucose levels. These foods are known as high glycemic index foods and should be avoided by people with diabetes. This doesn't mean you should not consumer starchy foods. There are better foods with a low glycemic level like whole grains, wild rice, and brown rice.

Proteins

We discussed proteins in our previous topic. One thing we can add is that diabetics, like other people, need to eat the correct amount of proteins. Besides, helping your muscles grow, proteins protect your heart health. As such, you should eat proteins every day. Primarily, aim at eating at most 2 portions of oily fish each week.

Oils And Spreads

As mentioned earlier, you need to eat less saturated fat. This way, you will lower cholesterol, hence curb the risk of stroke and heart disease.

Chapter 2: Crockpot 101

What is Crockpot?

In our cookbook, we'll reveal some of the most delicious meals you can cook using your crockpot. This is one of the most used kitchen appliances, and it comes in handy in the fall and winter.

So, do you really know what a crockpot is?

To better understand what a crockpot is, you must first understand what a slow cooker is. As the name suggests, a slow cooker is a kitchen appliance that cooks food slowly. In other words, a slow cooker uses moist heat to cook food, usually, over a long time. For example, cooking stew on a stove takes at most two hours, but with a slow cooker this can take up to 10 hours.

Now back to the crux of this topic, what is a crockpot. You will be surprised to know that a crockpot and a slow cooker perform the same function. They are multicookers that use electricity and moist heat for cooking food. As a result, they make foods super tender and integrate the flavors more strongly than in short-term cooking.

The name crockpot is a term trademarked by Rival Manufacturing Company when they introduced the cooker in 1971. Since this term is a registered trademark, the rival manufacturer opted to use the word "slow cooker" to avoid legal disputes. This gave birth to the slow cooker we see today.

Interestingly, all crockpots are slow cookers, but not all slow cookers are crockpots. So, what's the difference between a crockpot and a slow cooker? This is not the easiest topic in the world of kitchen appliances. In fact, it almost difficult to differentiate between the two. The reason is simple: both terms are used interchangeably. One difference is probably the design. The crockpot has a ceramic or porcelain pot inside, whereas the slow cooker has a metal pot. Besides, the crockpot has heating elements at the bottom and on the sides, which is not the case with slow cookers.

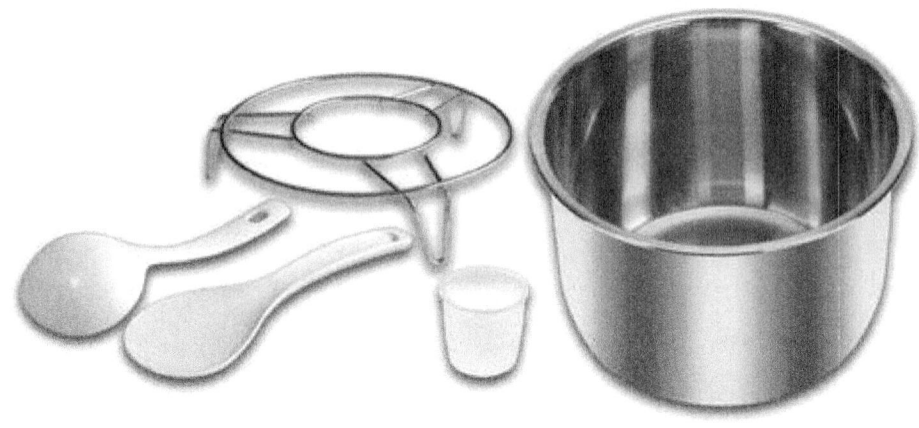

The Features And Functions of a Crock pot

A crockpot, like the slow cooker, has three main parts: the pot, the lid, and the heating elements.

Pot

In most cases, crockpots come with an oval ceramic pot. This shape makes it easy for the pot to accommodate large chunks of roasts and meat.

The Lid

The crockpot lid can be made of glass or clear plastic. The reason it's clear is to help you monitor the progress of the meal you are cooking without having to open the pot.

Other notable, crockpot functions include:

Heat Settings

Generally, crockpots have only two temperature settings. There is a LOW option that brings foods to temperatures, not above 200 degrees Fahrenheit. On the other hand, there is a HIGH option that brings food to a temperature of up to 300 degrees Fahrenheit. Some crockpot brands have a third temperature setting, a low-wattage, warming option.

Timer

Thanks to the advancement made in crockpots, it's possible to find brands with a timer. The time helps you to cook food for a specified period.

Tips For a Better Experience With a Crockpot

Since you will be using your crockpot to make all our recipes, its good you learn the tricks and tips to have an excellent experience with the appliance. Here are some tips to give you the best crockpot experience:

1. Always start by preheating your crockpot.
2. When cooking meat, start with room temperatures
3. For amazing flavors, add caramelized bits to the bottom of your crockpot.
4. For amazing texture, add gingerbread cookies when cooking meat dishes
5. Fill the pot two-thirds to three-quarters full.
6. Always trim fat from meat before cooking them in a crockpot.

Chapter 3: 21 Day Diabetic Meal Plan

Day	Breakfast	Lunch	Snack	Dinner
1	Lemon Berry Steel Cut Oats **Total Carbs: 35.2 g** Physical activity: walking	Tilapia Stew with Green Peppers **Total Carbs: 10 g**	Scotch Eggs **Total Carbs: 35.2 g**	Crockpot Turkey in Cream Sauce **Total Carbs: 6 g** Physical activity: jogging
2	Egg Casserole **Total Carbs: 20.8 g** Physical activity: Cycling	Chicken mushroom stew **Total Carbs: 0 g**	Crockpot turkey breasts **Total Carbs: 0 g**	Crockpot Black Bean Soup **Total Carbs: 35 g** Physical activity: yoga
3	Apple and Cinnamon Oatmeal **Total Carbs: 30.3g** Physical activity: Aerobic dancing	Lemon Pepper Salmon **Total Carbs: 15 g**	Pumpkin Muffins **Total Carbs: 15g**	Succulent Salmon with Caramelized Onions **Total Carbs: 7g** Physical activity: jogging
4	Cauliflower Oatmeal **Total Carbs: 16.3 g** Physical activity: Running	Tomato balsamic crockpot chicken **Total Carbs: 12 g**	No peel crockpot Hard-Boiled Eggs **Total Carbs: 1 g**	Sassy Pot Roast **Total Carbs: 10g** Physical activity: weight lifting
5	Breakfast Casserole **Total Carbs: 16.6 g** Physical activity: swimming	Almond Toffee Topped Pears **Total Carbs: 22 g**	Crockpot popcorns **Total Carbs: 14 g**	Chicken with Raisins, Capers and Basil **Total Carbs: 13 g** Physical activity: Calisthenics
6	Crockpot Breakfast Casserole **Total Carbs: 13.9 g** Physical activity: weight lifting	seafood Gumbo Stock **Total Carbs: 12.1 g**	Crockpot Deviled Eggs **Total Carbs: 1 g**	Shredded Green Chili Beef **Total Carbs: 14 g** Physical activity: Pilates
7	Spicy Breakfast Casserole	Hearty Cabbage Soup	Meatloaf on a sling **Total Carbs: 19 g**	Crockpot beefed-up vegetable stew

	Total Carbs: 38 g Physical activity: jogging	**Total Carbs: 15 g**		**Total Carbs: 14 g** Physical activity: swimming
8	Lemon Berry Steel Cut Oats **Total Carbs: 35.2 g** Physical activity: yoga	Poached Salmon **Total Carbs: 1 g**	Chipotle BBQ pork folded Tacos **Total Carbs: 15 g**	Turkey Breast with Gravy **Total Carbs: 2 g** Physical activity: Running
9	Cauliflower Oatmeal **Total Carbs: 16.3 g** Physical activity: Pilates	Caribbean curried chicken **Total Carbs: 11 g**	Vegetable Soup **Total Carbs: 30 g**	Chipotle Steak Simmer **Total Carbs: 13 g** Physical activity: Aerobic dancing
10	Apple and Cinnamon Oatmeal **Total Carbs: 30.3g** Physical activity: Calisthenics	chicken curry salad **Total Carbs: 17 g**	Egg and Vegetable Frittatas **Total Carbs: 15 g**	Pork and Pumpkin Stew **Total Carbs: 15 g** Physical activity: Cycling
11	Egg Casserole **Total Carbs: 20.8 g** Physical activity: walking	Asian Spaghetti Squash **Total Carbs: 21 g**	Flank Steak Tacos **Total Carbs: 13 g**	Turkey with Berry Compote **Total Carbs: 12 g** Physical activity: walking
12	Lemon Berry Steel Cut Oats **Total Carbs: 35.2 g** Physical activity: walking	Tilapia Stew with Green Peppers **Total Carbs: 10 g**	Scotch Eggs **Total Carbs: 35.2 g**	Crockpot Turkey in Cream Sauce **Total Carbs: 6 g** Physical activity: jogging
13	Egg Casserole **Total Carbs: 20.8 g** Physical activity: Cycling	Chicken mushroom stew **Total Carbs: 0 g**	Crockpot turkey breasts **Total Carbs: 0 g**	Crockpot Black Bean Soup **Total Carbs: 35 g** Physical activity: yoga
14	Apple and Cinnamon Oatmeal **Total Carbs: 30.3g** Physical activity: Aerobic dancing	Lemon Pepper Salmon **Total Carbs: 15 g**	Pumpkin Muffins **Total Carbs: 15g**	Succulent Salmon with Caramelized Onions **Total Carbs: 7g** Physical activity: jogging

15	Cauliflower Oatmeal **Total Carbs: 16.3 g** Physical activity: Running	Tomato balsamic crockpot chicken **Total Carbs: 12 g**	No peel crockpot Hard-Boiled Eggs **Total Carbs: 1 g**	Sassy Pot Roast **Total Carbs: 10g** Physical activity: weight lifting
16	Breakfast Casserole **Total Carbs: 16.6 g** Physical activity: swimming	Almond Toffee Topped Pears **Total Carbs: 22 g**	Crockpot popcorns **Total Carbs: 14 g**	Chicken with Raisins, Capers and Basil **Total Carbs: 13 g** Physical activity: Calisthenics
17	Crockpot Breakfast Casserole **Total Carbs: 13.9 g** Physical activity: weight lifting	seafood Gumbo Stock **Total Carbs: 12.1 g**	Crockpot Deviled Eggs **Total Carbs: 1 g**	Shredded Green Chili Beef **Total Carbs: 14 g** Physical activity: Pilates
18	Spicy Breakfast Casserole Total Carbs: 38 g Physical activity: jogging	Hearty Cabbage Soup **Total Carbs:15 g**	Meatloaf on a sling **Total Carbs: 19 g**	Crockpot beefed-up vegetable stew **Total Carbs: 14 g** Physical activity: swimming
19	Lemon Berry Steel Cut Oats **Total Carbs: 35.2 g** Physical activity: yoga	Poached Salmon **Total Carbs:1 g**	Chipotle BBQ pork folded Tacos **Total Carbs: 15 g**	Turkey Breast with Gravy **Total Carbs: 2 g** Physical activity: Running
20	Cauliflower Oatmeal **Total Carbs: 16.3 g** Physical activity: Pilates	Caribbean curried chicken **Total Carbs:11 g**	Vegetable Soup **Total Carbs: 30 g**	Chipotle Steak Simmer **Total Carbs: 13 g** Physical activity: Aerobic dancing
21	Apple and Cinnamon Oatmeal **Total Carbs: 30.3g** Physical activity: Calisthenics	chicken curry salad **Total Carbs:17 g**	Egg and Vegetable Frittatas **Total Carbs: 15 g**	Pork and Pumpkin Stew **Total Carbs: 15 g** Physical activity: Cycling

Chapter 4 Breakfast And Brunch

Dreamy Lemon Berry Steel Cut Oats

Prep time: 10 minutes, cook time: 5-8 hours; serves 2

Ingredients

1 cup steel-cut oats
1 tbsp pomegranate molasses
1 tbsp grated lemon zest
1 tbsp lemon juice
1 cup fresh strawberries and cranberries

What you'll need from store cupboard

1 tbsp olive oil
4 cups water
½ cup coconut milk
½ tbsp salt
¼ cup chia seeds

Instructions

1. Preheat your crockpot.
2. Meanwhile, sauté oil and oats, then toast in the crockpot, while stirring constantly.
3. Add water, milk, and molasses to the pot and mix together.
4. Add lemon zest, lemon juice, and salt, then stir to mix well.
5. Cover and cook for about 5-8 hours on low.
6. Add chia seeds and berries then mix well.
7. Allow the mixture to rest for a few minutes and serve with cow's cream.

Nutrition Facts Per Serving

Calories: 420, total fat: 17.5g, saturated fat: 3.3g, total carbs: 35.2g, net carbs: 24.6g, protein: 14.9g, sugars: 1.95g, fiber: 10.6g, sodium: 372mg, potassium: 161mg

Mouth-Watering Egg Casserole

Prep time: 15 minutes, cook time: 10 hours; serves 2

Ingredients
- 10oz ham, ½-inch slices
- ½ cup thinly sliced button mushrooms
- 1 tbsp seeded red capsicum, thinly sliced
- ¼ cup thawed artichoke hearts, frozen and quartered
- Whole basil leaves, fresh

What you'll need from store cupboard
- ¼ cup diced potatoes, cooked
- 1 tbsp drained tomatoes, sun-dried and chopped up
- ¼ cup thawed and drained spinach, chopped and frozen
- 10oz diced Swiss cheese
- 10oz goat feta cheese
- 2 eggs
- 1 cup whole milk
- 1 tbsp Dijon mustard
- Sea salt to taste
- Black pepper freshly cracked to taste

Instructions
1. Place a coated crockpot liner with cooking oil inside a crockpot, 2-qt
2. Grill the ham pieces for about 4 minutes until crisp. Retain the fat.
3. Sauté mushrooms and capsicum in the fat and butter for about 4 minutes until soft.
4. Place potatoes in the crockpot base and on top, then place an even layer of mushroom-capsicum mixture.
5. Add half of artichokes, tomatoes, and spinach in layers then sprinkle with half swiss cheese, followed by remaining vegetables, then remaining cheese and feta cheese.
6. Meanwhile, combine eggs, milk, and mustard in a bowl then pour over to settle through on the dish.
7. Place ham on top.
8. Cover and cook for about 8 hours on low then use the liner to remove the casserole.
9. Rest for about 10 minutes, then remove the liner.
10. Slice the casserole and garnish with basil leaves.
11. Serve alongside with green salad, leafy.

Nutrition Facts Per Serving
Calories: 297, total fat: 17g, saturated fat: 11g, total carbs: 20.8g, net carbs: 18.4g, protein: 15.8g, sugars: 10.2g, fiber: 2.4g, sodium: 416mg, potassium: 617mg

Wonderful Spicy Breakfast Casserole

Prep time: 10 minutes, cook time: 8 hours; serves 2

Ingredients

2 whole apples, medium and thinly sliced
1 cup natural muesli

What you' ll need from store cupboard

½ tbsp Cinnamon
1 tbsp butter, Unsalted

Instructions

1. Place the apples in a crockpot then add all the remaining ingredients.
2. Cover the pot and cook for about 8 hours.
3. Remove and serve with pure dairy cream.

Nutritional Information

Calories: 218, total fat: 7g, saturated fat: 2g, total carbs: 38g, net carbs: 34g, protein: 3g, sugars: 9.5g, fiber: 4g, sodium: 15mg, potassium: 181mg

Amazing Overnight Apple and Cinnamon Oatmeal

Prep time: 10 minutes, cook time: 7 hours; serves 2

Ingredients

¾ cup coconut milk
1 diced whole apple
½ cup steel cut oats
½ tbsp raw honey

What you'll need from store cupboard

1 tbsp coconut oil
¾ cup water, fresh
¼ tbsp salt to taste, sea
1 tbsp cinnamon

Instructions

1. Spray your crockpot with cooking oil. This is to prevent food from sticking.
2. Add water, coconut milk, apples, oats, coconut oil, raw honey, salt, and cinnamon. Stir to combine.
3. Cover and cook for about 6-7 hours on low.
4. Serve hot with favorite toppings.

Nutrition Facts Per Serving

Calories: 284, total fat: 17.9g, saturated fat: 15g, total carbs: 30.3g, net carbs: 25.6g, protein: 4.2g, sugars: 1.3g, fiber: 4.7g, sodium: 30mg, potassium: 90mg

Apple Cinnamon Oatmeal

Prep time: 10, cook time: 8 hours; serves 4

Ingredients

2 peeled and sliced apples
1 tbsp cinnamon
⅓ Cup brown sugar
2 cups rolled oats, old-fashioned

What you'll need from store cupboard

Pinch of salt
4 cups water

Instructions

1. Place the apples in the crockpot bottom then add cinnamon and sugar over the apples. Stir to mix.
2. Add the oats over apples evenly then add salt and water. Do not stir.
3. Cover and cook for about 8-9 hours on low or cook overnight.
4. Stir well, making sure oats are not at the bottom.
5. Serve.

Nutrition Facts Per Serving

Calories: 232.4, total fat: 3.1g, saturated fat: 1g, total carbs: 53g, net carbs: 47g, protein: 5.2g, sugars: 20.9g, fiber: 6g, sodium: 4.9mg, potassium: 263mg

Breakfast Casserole

Prep time: 10 minutes, cook time: 10 hours; serves 12

Ingredients

32 ounces hash browns, frozen
1 lb cubed lean ham, cooked
1½ cups of cheese, shredded
1 cup skim milk

What you'll need from store cupboard

2 Onions
1 tbsp black pepper
12 eggs
1 tbsp salt

Instructions

1. Prepare your crockpot by spraying with cooking oil.
2. Divide the ham, potatoes, cheese, and veggies to create several layers in the crockpot of each.
3. To create layers, add hash browns, then ham, then onions, then pepper and lastly cheese. Repeat for several layers.
4. Beat eggs, pepper, salt, and milk over the layers. Cover the crockpot.
5. Cook for about 10-12 hours or overnight.
6. Serve.

Nutrition Facts Per Serving

Calories: 2228.8, total fat: 11.6g, saturated fat: 7g, total carbs: 16.6g, net carbs: 16.1g, protein: 14.7g, sugars: 1.4g, fiber: 0.5g, sodium: 735.2mg, potassium: 414.5mg

Cauliflower Oatmeal

Prep time: 5 minutes, cook time: 10 minutes; serves 1

Ingredients
1 cup cauliflower rice
½ cup almond milk, unsweetened
1 sliced strawberry

What you'll need from store cupboard
¼ tbsp stevia
½ tbsp cinnamon
½ tbsp peanut butter

Instructions
1. Place the rice in a crockpot then add milk, stevia, and cinnamon. Boil over high heat while stirring.
2. Reduce heat to low and continue to boil for about 8-10 minutes while stirring.
3. Add more milk if too thick and transfer to a bowl.
4. Drizzle the cauliflower oatmeal with peanut butter then top with strawberry slices.
5. Serve and enjoy.

Nutrition Facts Per Serving
Calories: 139, total fat: 6.6g, saturated fat: 0.8g, total carbs: 16.3g, net carbs: 9g, protein: 6.8g, sugars: 5.8g, fiber: 7.3g, sodium: 230.3g, potassium: 217.3mg

Crockpot Breakfast Casserole

Prep time: 15 minutes, cook time: 6 hours serves 8

Ingredients
16-ounce frozen potatoes, hash brown
½ pound bacon, cooked and diced
½ cup diced mushrooms
2 cups milk

What you will need from store cupboard
2 cups cheddar cheese, shredded
½ cup onion, chopped
10 eggs, large
Pepper to taste
Salt to taste

Instructions
1. Place potatoes, cheese, onion, bacon, and mushrooms in a bowl. Stir together.
2. Add pepper and salt, then place in a crockpot. Make sure the crockpot is prepared by spraying cooking oil.
3. Whisk eggs and milk together then pour over mixture in the crockpot — season with pepper and salt.
4. Cover the crockpot and cook for about 6-7 hours. Ensure the eggs are set.
5. Serve and enjoy.

Nutrition Facts Per Serving
Calories: 419 total fat: 28g saturated fat: 12.3g total carbs: 13.9g net carbs: 12.3g protein: 27.6g sugars: 4.4g fiber: 1.6g sodium: 959mg potassium: 552mg

Chapter 5 Vegan And Vegetable

Vegetable Soup

Prep time: 35 minutes, cook time: 5 hours; Serves 2

Ingredients

14 oz canned tomatoes, with no salt, added
2 carrots
1 medium parsnip, diced
1 red bell pepper, seeded and diced
1 tbsp spike seasoning

What you'll need from the store cupboard

1 onion, diced
4 garlic cloves, minced
2 celery stalks, diced
6 cups vegetable broth, low sodium
3 cups cabbage, chopped
½ tbsp salt
¼ tbsp black pepper
1 sweet potato, peeled and diced

Instructions

1. Add all the ingredients in a crockpot.
2. Set the timer for five hours on high.
3. When time elapses, stir, mash the parsnips, and sweet potatoes to thicken the soup.
4. Serve and enjoy when hot.

Nutrition Facts Per Serving

Calories 135, Total Fat 0.5g, Saturated Fat 0g, Total Carbs 30g, Net Carbs 20g, Protein 4g, Sugar 14g, Fiber 7g, Sodium 250mg, Potassium 880 mg

Almond Toffee Topped Pears

Prep time: 35 minutes, cook time: 5 hours; Serves 2

Ingredients

¼ almonds, silvered
8 caramel-flavored hard candies, sugar-free and crushed
1 cinnamon stick
2 pears, firm
½ tbsp vanilla extract

What you'll need from the store cupboard

1 pinch salt
¼ cup apple juice
¾ Cup water
1 tbsp light butter with canola oil

Instructions

1. Heat the crockpot until hot and add the almonds. Stir cook for four minutes. Set aside, then chop them.
2. Add the almonds in a small mixing bowl and add candies and salt.
3. Place apple juice, water, and cinnamon stick in the crockpot. Place a steamer basket in place and arrange the pears.
4. Cover the crockpot and cook for five minutes on high pressure.
5. Remove the pears from the crockpot and cut them side up.
6. Remove the cinnamon stick and boil the cooking liquid. Boil until the liquid is reduced to a quarter cup.
7. Stir in candy mixture, vanilla extract, and butter. Stir cook until the toffee melts.
8. Spoon about four tablespoons of the sauce on each pear half. Serve and enjoy.

Nutrition Facts Per Serving

Calories 130, Total Fat 5g, Saturated Fat 1g, Total Carbs 22g, Net Carbs 17g, Protein 2g, Sugar 11g, Fiber 4g, Sodium 80mg, Potassium 170 mg

Hearty Cabbage Soup

Prep time: 20 minutes, cook time: 1 hour; Serves 9

Ingredients

2 carrots, diced
2 celery stalks, diced
½ lb. turkey breakfast sausage, lean
40 oz chicken broth, low sodium
15 ½ Great northern beans

What you'll need from the store cupboard

Cooking spray
1 onion, diced
½ cabbage chopped
14 ½ tomato, diced
¼ tbsp black pepper
½ tbsp dried oregano

Instructions

1. Spray your crockpot with cooking spray and set to low
2. Add onion, carrots, and celery, and sauté until onions are clear.
3. Remove from pot and set aside. Add turkey sausage to the crockpot and cook on high until browned.
4. Add the onion mixture and mix well. Add all the remaining ingredients and bring to boil.
5. Cover the crockpot and simmer at low for ten minutes.
6. Serve and enjoy.

Nutrition Facts Per Serving

Calories 120, Total Fat 2.5g, Saturated Fat 1g, Total Carbs 15g, Net Carbs 10g, Protein 10g, Sugar 9g, Fiber 5g, Sodium 360mg, Potassium 550 mg

Vegan Thai Mushroom Soup

Prep time: 20 minutes, cook time: 45 minutes; Serves 4

Ingredients

8 oz Cremini mushrooms, sliced
15 oz chickpeas, no added salt
1 tbsp sriracha
½ tbsp cumin, ground
1 ½ cup lite coconut milk

What you'll need from the store cupboard

Pepper and onion blend, frozen
14 ½ oz tomatoes, diced
½ cup water
½ cup cilantro
1 tbsp ginger, fresh
½ tbsp salt

Instructions

1. Add mushrooms, pepper and onion blend, chickpeas, diced tomatoes, sriracha, cumin, and water in the crockpot.
2. Cover the crockpot and cook for eight minutes on high.
3. When the time elapses, remove the lid and stir in the remaining ingredients.
4. Let rest for five minutes to allow the flavors to blend.
5. Serve and enjoy when warm.

Nutrition Facts Per Serving

Calories 240, Total Fat 7g, Saturated Fat 5g, Total Carbs 7g, Net Carbs 28g, Protein 12g, Sugar 8g, Fiber 7g, Sodium 440mg, Potassium 930 mg

Individual Egg and Vegetable Frittatas

Prep time: 35 minutes, cook time: 5 hours; Serves 4

Ingredients

1 ⅓ cups corn kernels, frozen
1 cup kale, chopped
1 cup red bell pepper, chopped
1 cup green onion, chopped
¼ tbsp dried thyme

What you'll need from the store cupboard

Cooking spray
4 eggs
4 egg whites
¼ tbsp salt
1 cup water
2 oz cheddar cheese, reduced-fat

Instructions

1. Coat four ramekins with cooking spray and divide the kernels, kale, pepper, and green onions among the ramekins.
2. Pack the veggies by pressing using a spoon back.
3. In a mixing bowl, whisk together eggs, egg whites, salt, and thyme. Carefully pour over each ramekin.
4. Coat a paper foil with cooking spray and cover the ramekins individually.
5. Add water to the crockpot and place a trivet in place. Place the ramekins on the trivet and stack the fourth ramekin on the other ramekins.
6. Set the timer for ten minutes on high. When time elapses, remove lid and remove the ramekins from the crockpot.
7. Remove the foil from the ramekins and sprinkle with more salt and cheese. Let rest for peak flavors.
8. Serve and enjoy.

Nutrition Facts Per Serving

Calories 200, Total Fat 8g, Saturated Fat 3g, Total Carbs 15g, Net Carbs 11g, Protein 16g, Sugar 5g, Fiber 3g, Sodium 440mg, Potassium 410 mg

Chicken Curry Salad

Prep time: 35 minutes, cook time: 5 hours; Serves 2

Ingredients

12 oz chicken breasts, boneless and skinless
¼ cup plain Greek yogurt
¼ cup light mayonnaise
2 cup asparagus, cut into one inch
1 cup shelled edamame, frozen

What you'll need from the store cupboard

¼ tbsp black pepper
1 tbsp cumin, ground
2 cups water
1 ½ tbsp curry powder
½ tbsp salt
Baby kale mix
½ cup red onion, chopped
¼ cup green onion or cilantro, chopped

Instructions

1. Sprinkle the chicken breast with black pepper and cumin.
2. Add water to the crockpot and place a steamer basket. Arrange the chicken breasts on the steamer basket.
3. Lid the crockpot and set the timer for ten minutes. When time is done remove chicken from crockpot and place it on a cutting board. Let rest before slicing to your desired pieces sizes.
4. Whisk together yogurt, mayo, curry powder, and salt, then set aside.
5. Place the asparagus and shelled edamame on the steamer basket. Lid the crockpot and set the timer for one minute.
6. Transfer the asparagus to a colander then run under cold water. Drain well.
7. Divide the kale among four dinner plates and top with the asparagus mixture.
8. Add the chicken pieces, onions, yogurt dressing in another mixing bowl, and toss to coat.
9. Divide the chicken mixture among the veggie plates. Sprinkle cilantro and serve.
10. Enjoy.

Nutrition Facts Per Serving

Calories 240, Total Fat 8g, Saturated Fat 1.5 g, Total Carbs 17g, Net Carbs 12g, Protein 26g, Sugar 8g, Fiber 5g, Sodium 470mg, Potassium 660 mg

Asian Spaghetti Squash

Prep time: 20 minutes, cook time: 7 hours; Serves 6

Ingredients

3 lb. spaghetti squash

3 tbsp soy sauce, low sodium

12 oz shelled edamame, frozen

1 cup matchstick carrots

What you'll need from the store cupboard

1 cup water

2 limes

4 tbsp sugar

⅛ tbsp red pepper flakes, crushed

1 tbsp ginger, grated

½ cup green onions, chopped

½ fresh cilantro, chopped

Instructions

1. Use a knife to pierce the entire surface of the squash. Place the squash in the microwave to cook for two minutes.
2. Remove the squash from the microwave and cut it crosswise. Remove the seeds and the connecting strands.
3. Pour water in the crockpot and place the two squash halves on the trivet. Cover the crockpot and cook for seven minutes.
4. Meanwhile, combine soy sauce, one lime juice, sugar, pepper, and ginger in a mixing bowl. Mix until well incorporated.
5. When the time is done, remove the squash from the crockpot and place it on a cutting board.
6. Add the shelled edamame to the cooking liquid and bring it to boil. Let it boil for two minutes then drain well.
7. Run a fork around the squash outer edges to release spaghetti squash strands.
8. Divide the squash among six bowls and top with edamame, soy sauce mixture, carrots, onions, and sprinkle with cilantro.
9. Cut the remaining limes into six equal pieces and place them on each bowl.
10. Serve and enjoy.

Nutrition Facts Per Serving

Calories 180, Total Fat 8g, Saturated Fat 0.5g, Total Carbs 21g, Net Carbs 15g, Protein 10g, Sugar 9g, Fiber 6g, Sodium 320mg, Potassium 820 mg

Easy Black Bean Soup

Prep time: 15 minutes, cook time: 6 hours; Serves 8

Ingredients

28 oz can tomato, diced and undrained
38 oz can black beans, drained and rinsed
2 ½ cubes McCormick's vegetable Bouillon
2 cups green beans, frozen

What you'll need from the store cupboard

1 onion, chopped
4 garlic cloves, crushed
2 tbsp cumin, ground
2 tbsp ginger, ground
2 tbsp curry powder

Instructions

1. Add all ingredients in your crockpot except the bouillon cubes.
2. Dissolve the bouillon cubes in hot water and add to the crockpot.
3. Add water to your desired level.
4. Set timer for seven hours. When time elapses, put in serving cups; two cups per serving.
5. Enjoy.

Nutrition Facts Per Serving

Calories 210, Total Fat 1.8g, Saturated Fat 0g, Total Carbs 35g, Net Carbs 28g, Protein 12.2g, Sugar 8g, Fiber 9.2g, Sodium 1323mg, Potassium 980 mg

Chapter 6 Fish And Seafood

Tilapia Stew with Green Peppers

Prep time: 40 minutes, cook time: 15 minutes; Serves 4

Ingredients
1 green bell pepper, medium
1 can stewed tomatoes, with Italian seasoning
1 lb tilapia
½ tbsp seafood seasoning

What you'll need from the store cupboard
1 cup water
Cooking spray, nonstick

Instructions
1. Coat your crockpot with cooking spray. Add bell peppers and sauté until lightly brown.
2. Add the tomatoes then simmer until they are tender. Break down the large pieces of the tomatoes.
3. Add tilapia to the pot and stir gently. Lid the crockpot and bring to boil. Reduce heat so that the fish simmers for about three minutes.
4. Remove from heat and let sit for about ten minutes for peak flavors. Serve and enjoy.

Nutrition Facts Per Serving
Calories 150, Total Fat 2g, Saturated Fat 0.5g, Total Carbs 10g, Net Carbs 7g, Protein 24g, Sugar 6g, Fiber 2g, Sodium 350mg, Potassium 620mg

Succulent Salmon with Caramelized Onions

Prep time: 15 minutes, cook time: 20 minutes; Serves 4

Ingredients

1 lb salmon
½ sweet onion
¼ tbsp ginger, ground
¼ tbsp dried dill
½ lemon, sliced

What you'll need from the store cupboard

1 tbsp olive oil
¼ salt
⅛ tbsp pepper

Instructions

1. Cut salmon into desired pieces, and that will fit into the crockpot.
2. Place the onions at the bottom of the crockpot. Foil each salmon piece in a different paper foil enough to be folded like a packet.
3. Sprinkle spices over the salmon pieces and top with lemon. Fold the paper foil into packets and stack them on the onions.
4. Set the timer for six hours on low. When the time elapses, remove the salmon from packets and top with onions.
5. Serve and enjoy.

Nutrition Facts Per Serving

Calories 215, Total Fat 11g, Saturated Fat 2g, Total Carbs 7g, Net Carbs 5g, Protein 24g, Sugar 3g, Fiber 2g, Sodium 200mg, Potassium 520mg

Seafood Gumbo Stock

Prep time: 15 minutes, cook time: 7 hours 30 minutes; Serves 8

Ingredients

1 lb shrimp shells
4 carrots, sliced
½ bunch celery, sliced
2 bay leaves
2 sprigs parsley, fresh

What you' ll need from the store cupboard

5 cups water
4 onions
3 garlic cloves, sliced
5 garlic cloves, whole
1 tbsp black pepper, ground
1 tbsp dried basil
2 tbsp dried thyme

Instructions

1. Preheat oven to 3750F.
2. Bake the shrimps until the edges start to brown.
3. Add all the ingredients to the crockpot and bring to boil.
4. Reduce heat, lid, and set time for six hours. Replace water two to three times as needed.
5. Remove stock from the crockpot and strain. Press liquid from all shells and vegetables then discard them.
6. Return stock to the crockpot and heat until it is reduced to eight cups.
7. Serve and enjoy.

Nutrition Facts Per Serving

Calories 112, Total Fat 1.3g, Saturated Fat 0g, Total Carbs 12.1g, Net Carbs 9g, Protein 13.2g, Sugar 5g, Fiber 3.3g, Sodium 162mg, Potassium 464mg

Simple Poached Salmon

Prep time: 10 minutes, cook time: 1 hour 20 minutes; Serves 4

Ingredients

1 onion, sliced1 celery rib, sliced
1 carrot, sliced
3 thyme sprigs, fresh
1 rosemary sprig, fresh
24 oz salmon fillet

What you'll need from the store cupboard

2 cups water
1 cup white wine
2 tbsp lemon juice
1 bay leaf
½ tbsp salt
¼ tbsp pepper
Lemon wedges

Instructions

1. Add all the ingredients in your crockpot except salmon and lemon wedges.
2. Place the lid and set time for forty-five minutes.
3. When time elapses, add the salmon fillets and add water until the salmon is covered.
4. Cook until the salmon easily flakes or for forty-five minutes.
5. Remove fish from cooking liquids and serve with lemon wedges. Enjoy

Nutrition Facts Per Serving

Calories 272, Total Fat 16g, Saturated Fat 3g, Total Carbs 1g, Net Carbs 0g, Protein 29g, Sugar 0g, Fiber 0g, Sodium 115mg, Potassium 320mg

Sophia Homemade Crockpot Seafood Stock

Prep time: 20 minutes, cook time: 4 hours 20 minutes; Serves 10

Ingredients
4 carrots, coarsely chopped
1 bunch celery, coarsely chopped
2 green bell peppers, coarsely chopped
½ lb fish parts, bones and tail + 2 fish heads
2 cups clam juice

What you'll need from the store cupboard
1 tbsp olive oil
2 onions, coarsely chopped
1 bunch cilantro, fresh
½ bunch oregano, fresh
2 bay leaves
1 ½ bottles water
1 tbsp whole black peppercorns

Instructions
1. Heat olive oil in your crockpot. Stir cook onions for five minutes then add carrots, celery, and peppers.
2. Sauté for five more minutes, then add the spices. Sauté for two additional minutes.
3. Add water, fish parts and heads, clam juice, and peppercorns to the crockpot.
4. Bring mixture to boil then cook on low for four hours. Turn off the heat and let rest for thirty minutes.
5. Strain the stock using a fine mesh strainer so that all fish bones are removed.
6. Serve and enjoy.

Nutrition Facts Per Serving
Calories 55, Total Fat 1.7g, Saturated Fat 0g, Total Carbs 9.2g, Net Carbs 6.4g, Protein 1.6g, Sugar 4g, Fiber 2.8g, Sodium 182mg, Potassium 446mg

10-minute Crockpot Salmon

Prep time: 5 minutes, cook time: 5minutes; Serves 4

Ingredients

3 lemon
4 salmon fillets
1 bunch fresh dill weed

What you' ll need from the store cupboard

¾ cup water
1 tbsp butter, unsalted
¼ tbsp salt
¼ tbsp ground black pepper

Instructions

1. Add a quarter cup lemon juice with three quarter cup water to the crockpot.
2. Place a steamer basket in place and place the salmon fillets on top.
3. Sprinkle dill weed and place a lemon slice on each salmon fillet.
4. Lid the crockpot and set time for five minutes. Remove the salmon from the crockpot and serve with butter, more dill, and lemon, salt, and pepper to taste. Enjoy.

Nutrition Facts Per Serving

Calories 441, Total Fat 30g, Saturated Fat 9g, Total Carbs 12g, Net Carbs 8g, Protein 36g, Sugar 3g, Fiber 4g, Sodium 402mg, Potassium 426mg

Lemon Pepper Salmon

Prep time: 5 minutes, cook time: 10 minutes; Serves 4

Ingredients

1 lb salmon fillet with skin
3 tbsp ghee
½ lemon, thinly sliced

What you'll need from the store cupboard

¾ cups water
2 sprigs basil
¼ tbsp salt
½ tbsp pepper
1 zucchini, julienned
1 red bell pepper, julienned
1 carrot, julienned

Instructions

1. Pour water and all the herbs in your crockpot. Place the steamer basket.
2. Place the salmon fillet on the steamer basket with the skin side down.
3. Drizzle ghee and season with salt and pepper. Cover the salmon fillets with lemon slices.
4. Lid the crockpot and set time for three minutes. Carefully remove the steamer basket from the crockpot and discard the herbs.
5. Add the vegetables and let them cook for two minutes.
6. Serve the salmon with veggies and enjoy.

Nutrition Facts Per Serving

Calories 296, Total Fat 15g, Saturated Fat 4g, Total Carbs 8g, Net Carbs 5g, Protein 31g, Sugar 4g, Fiber 2g, Sodium 284mg, Potassium 1084mg

Simple Steamed Crab Legs

Prep time: 5 minutes, cook time: 15 minutes; Serves 4

Ingredients
2 lb king crab legs, frozen
1 lemon juice
⅓ Cup melted butter

What you'll need from the store cupboard
1 ½ cups water

Instructions
1. Place the trivet in the crockpot then add water. Place the crab legs on the trivet; thaw them first if they do not fit the crockpot.
2. Set the timer for ten minutes on high pressure. When time is done, remove the crab legs from the crockpot.
3. Sprinkle lemon juice on top and serve with melted butter. Enjoy.

Nutrition Facts Per Serving
Calories 199, Total Fat 16g, Saturated Fat 10g, Total Carbs 1.2g, Net Carbs 0g, Protein 12.7g, Sugar 0g, Fiber 0g, Sodium 324mg, Potassium 244mg

Chapter 7 Poultry

Chicken Noodle Soup

Prep time: 20 minutes, cook time: 5 hours; Serves 6

Ingredients

12 baby carrots, fresh
4 celery ribs
1 tbsp parsley, minced
1 ¼ lb chicken breast halves and thighs each, boneless and skinless
14 ½ oz chicken broth

What you'll need from the store cupboard

¾ cup onions, finely chopped
½ tbsp pepper
¼ tbsp cayenne pepper
1 tbsp mustard seed
2 peeled and halved garlic cloves
9 oz refrigerated linguine
Pepper to taste, coarsely ground

Instructions

1. Add carrots, celery ribs, onion, parsley, pepper, and cayenne pepper in a crockpot.
2. Put mustard seed and garlic in a spice bag with a double thickness and add to the crockpot.
3. Add chicken breast, thigh, and broth to the pot, cover, and set the timer for six hours.
4. When time elapses, remove the chicken from the crockpot and place it on a chopping board. Discard the spice bag.
5. Stir in the linguine, cover, and cook for thirty minutes.
6. Cut the chicken into pieces and add it to the soup. Heat through and sprinkle ground pepper into the soup.
7. Serve and enjoy.

Nutrition Facts Per Serving

Calories 199, Total Fat 6g, Saturated Fat 2g, Total Carbs 14g, Net Carbs 11g, Protein 22g, Sugar 2g, Fiber 1g, Sodium 663mg

Chicken Mushroom Stew

Prep time: 20 minutes, cook time: 5 hours 45 minutes; Serves 6

Ingredients
6 chicken breast halves, boneless and skinless
8 oz fresh sliced mushroom
3 cups zucchini, diced
1 cup green pepper, chopped

What you'll need from the store cupboard
2 tbsp divided canola oil
1 diced medium onion
4 minced garlic cloves
3 chopped medium tomatoes
6 oz tomato paste
¾ cup water
2 tbsp each dried basil
2 tbsp thyme
2 tbsp marjoram
2 tbsp oregano

Instructions
1. Cut the chicken into small cubes and place it in a skillet.
2. Brown the chicken with one tablespoon oil and transfer into a crockpot.
3. Using the same skillet sauté, the mushroom, onion, zucchini, and green pepper in remaining oil until they become tender-crisp then transfer the mixture to the crockpot.
4. Add garlic to the crockpot and cook for one minute.
5. Transfer the mixture into the crockpot and add tomatoes, tomato paste, water, basil, thyme, marjoram, and oregano.
6. cover and cook for five hours
7. Serve and enjoy.

Nutrition Facts Per Serving
Calories 237, Total Fat 8g, Saturated Fat 1g, Total Carbs 15g, Net Carbs 12g, Protein 27g, Sugar 7g, Fiber 3g, Sodium 82mg

Tomato Balsamic Crockpot Chicken

Prep time: 25 minutes, cook time: 7 hours; Serves 6

Ingredients

2 chopped medium carrots
2lb chicken thighs, bone-in and skinless
½ cup chicken broth, reduced-sodium
1 bay leaf
Orzo, hot cooked

What you'll need from the store cupboard

½ cup shallot, sliced
1tbsp flour, all-purpose
14½ oz tomatoes, diced and undrained
¼ cup vinegar, balsamic
1tbsp olive oil
2 minced garlic cloves
½ tbsp Italian seasoning
½ tbsp salt
¼ tbsp pepper

Instructions

1. Put carrots and shallots in a crockpot and place the chicken on top.
2. Whisk flour and broth in a bowl until smooth, then stir in tomatoes, vinegar, oil, garlic, bay leaf, and seasoning.
3. Pour the mixture in the bowl over the chicken, cover, and cook for seven hours.
4. When time is done, remove the chicken and place it on a chopping board and discard bay leaf
5. Remove the bones from chicken bones and return it to the crockpot then heat through.
6. Serve with orzo and enjoy

Nutrition Facts Per Serving

Calories 235, Total Fat 11g, Saturated Fat 3g, Total Carbs 12g, Net Carbs 10g, Protein 23g, Sugar 7g, Fiber 2g, Sodium 433mg

Turkey in Cream Sauce

Prep time: 20 minutes, cook time: 8 hours 15 minutes; Serves 8

Ingredients

1 ¼ cups white wine
2 bay leaves
2 tbsp crushed and dried rosemary
¾ lb turkey breast tenderloins each
½ cup whole or cream

What you' ll need from the store cupboard

1 chopped medium onion
2 minced garlic cloves
½ tbsp pepper
3 tbsp cornstarch
½ tbsp salt

Instructions

1. Add wine, onion, garlic, and bay leaves in a crockpot.
2. Mix rosemary and pepper in a bowl, then rub over the turkey and put them in the crockpot.
3. Cover the crockpot and cook for eight hours.
4. When time is done, remove the turkey and put it in a serving platter
5. Skim fat from cooking juice, put the juice in a saucepan and heat to boil.
6. In the hot liquid stir in cornstarch, cream, and salt and allow it boil it for two minutes.
7. Serve with turkey and enjoy it.

Nutrition Facts Per Serving

Calories 205, Total Fat 3g, Saturated Fat 1g, Total Carbs 6g, Net Carbs 5g, Protein 32g, Sugar 1g, Fiber 0g, Sodium 231mg

Slow Simmered Crockpot Chicken with Raisins, Capers and Basil

Prep time: 25 minutes, cook time: 5 hours; Serves 8

Ingredients

4oz chicken thigh, boneless, skinless, and cut into 8 pieces
8 oz mushrooms, sliced
½ cup golden raisins
¼ cup basil, chopped
Hot cooked couscous

What you'll need from the store cupboard

2 tbsp divided olive oil
1 tbsp salt
1 tbsp pepper
½ cup marsala wine
1 sliced medium sweet red pepper
1 sliced medium onion
14 ½ tomatoes, diced

Instructions

1. Heat one tablespoon oil in a skillet.
2. Spread the chicken on a chopping board and sprinkle it with salt and pepper.
3. Brown the chicken with oil and transfer it to a crockpot.
4. Stir in the wine in the skillet to loosen the bits and add it to the crockpot.
5. Stir in mushrooms, red pepper, onion, and tomatoes to the crockpot.
6. Cover the crockpot and cook for five hours.
7. Sprinkle the delicacy with basil.
8. Serve with couscous and enjoy.

Nutrition Facts Per Serving

Calories 250, Total Fat 12g, Saturated Fat 3g, Total Carbs 13g, Net Carbs 11g, Protein 23g, Sugar 9g, Fiber 2g, Sodium 494mg

Turkey Breast with Gravy

Prep time: 20 minutes, cook time: 6 hours 15 minutes; Serves 12

Ingredients
2 tbsp parsley, dried and in flakes
1 tbsp poultry seasoning
3 medium carrots
3 chopped celery ribs
6 lb bone-in and skinless turkey breast

What you'll need from the store cupboard
1 tbsp salt
½ tbsp paprika
½ tbsp pepper
2 chopped medium onions
½ cup all-purpose flour
½ cup water

Instructions
1. Mix parsley, salt, poultry seasoning, paprika and pepper in a bowl
2. Put the onions, carrots, and celery in a crockpot and place the turkey on top.
3. Rub the turkey with the seasoning mixture in the bowl.
4. Cover and cook for six hours.
5. Remove turkey from the crockpot and put it on a chopping board and slice it after fifteen minutes.
6. Put cooking juices into a saucepan.
7. In another bowl, mix flour and water until they become smooth then stir in the mixture into the cooking juices.
8. Heat the mixture as you stir and allow it to boil for two minutes.
9. Serve with the turkey and enjoy it.

Nutrition Facts Per Serving
Calories 200, Total Fat 1g, Saturated Fat 0g, Total Carbs 2g, Net Carbs 2g, Protein 43g, Sugar 0g, Fiber 0g, Sodium 270mg

Caribbean Curried Chicken

Prep time: 20 minutes, cook time: 6 hours 15 minutes; Serves 8

Ingredients

1 tbsp madras curry powder
4 0z chicken thigh boneless and skinless
1 sliced medium onion
1 ½ cups Goya mojo Criollo marinade

What you'll need from the store cupboard

1 tbsp garlic powder
1 tbsp pepper
1 tbsp canola oil
2 tbsp all-purpose flour
Green onions for serving
Cilantro leaves for serving

Instructions

1. Mix madras curry powder, garlic powder, and pepper in a bowl and sprinkle it over chicken as you press so that it can adhere properly.
2. Put the chicken in a crockpot and sprinkle onions on it.
3. Pour mojo criollo marinade on the sides of the crockpot avoiding contact with the chicken.
4. Cover and cook for six hours.
5. Remove the chicken from heat and put it in a hot dish.
6. Put cooking juice from the crockpot in a cup and skim fat.
7. In a saucepan, pour oil and heat it as you whisk in flour until smooth.
8. Pour the cooking juices into the mixture.
9. Stir cook the mixture and allow it to boil for two minutes so that the mixture thickens.
10. Add the chicken into the mixture and simmer for five minutes.
11. Serve with rice, green onions, and cilantro and enjoy.

Nutrition Facts Per Serving

Calories 249, Total Fat 13g, Saturated Fat 3g, Total Carbs 11g, Net Carbs 10g, Protein 22g, Sugar 5g, Fiber 1g, Sodium 514mg

Turkey with Berry Compote

Prep time: 35minutes, cook time:4 hours 20 minutes; Serves 12

Ingredients
½ tbsp thyme, dried
½ tbsp pepper
2 cups raspberries
2 cups blueberries
1 cup grape juice, white

What you'll need from the store cupboard
1 tbsp salt
½ tbsp garlic powder
½ tbsp pepper
⅓ Cup water
2 peeled and chopped medium apples
¼ tbsp red pepper, crushed and in flakes
¼ tbsp ginger, ground

Instructions
1. In a bowl, mix salt, garlic powder, thyme, and pepper and rub the turkey with the mixture
2. Put the turkey on a crockpot and pour water on the turkey.
3. Cover and cook for four hours.
4. When time elapses, remove the turkey from crockpot and put it on a chopping board.
5. Cover the turkey with foil and allow it to rest for ten minutes, then slice it.
6. Combine apples, raspberries, blueberries, grape juice red pepper, and ginger in a saucepan.
7. Cook the compote ingredients as you stir until the mixture thickens, and the apple become tender for twenty minutes.
8. Serve with turkey and enjoy it.

Nutrition Facts Per Serving
Calories 215, Total Fat 1g, Saturated Fat 0g, Total Carbs 12g, Net Carbs 10g, Protein 38g, Sugar 8g, Fiber 2g, Sodium 272mg

Chapter 8 Beef Lamb And Pork

Slow-cooked Flank Steak

Prep time: 15 minutes, cook time: 4 hours; serves 6

Ingredients

1 tbsp canola oil
1½ pounds flank steak
4 ounces green chilies, chopped
1¼ tbsp chili powder
1 tbsp garlic powder

What you'll need from store cupboard

1 sliced onion, large
⅓ Cup water
2 tbsp vinegar
½ tbsp sugar
½ tbsp salt
⅛ tbsp pepper

Instructions

1. Pour the oil in a skillet, then add steak and cook until brown. Transfer to a crockpot.
2. Now sauté the onion in the skillet for about 1 minute.
3. Add water gradually while stirring. This is to loosen brown bits out of the pan.
4. Add the rest of the ingredients then boil.
5. Pour over the browned steak.
6. Cover the crockpot then cook for about 4-5 hours on low until the steak is tender.
7. Slice the flank steak.
8. Serve with pan juices and onion.

Nutrition Facts Per Serving

Calories: 199, total fat: 11g, saturated fat: 4g, total carbs: 4g, net carbs: 3g, protein: 20g, sugars: 3g, fiber: 1g, sodium: 327mg, potassium: 756mg

Sassy Pot Roast

Prep time: 15 Minutes, Cook time: 8 hours; serves 8

Ingredients

2 pounds beef chuck roast
1 tbsp Worcestershire sauce
8 ounces tomato sauce
2 tbsp brown sugar
¼ cup ketchup

What you'll need from store cupboard

½ tbsp pepper
½ tbsp salt
1 chopped onion, large
¼ cup lemon juice
¼ cup cider vinegar
2 tbsp olive oil
¼ cup water
½ tbsp mustard, ground
½ tbsp paprika

Instructions

1. Splash the beef with pepper and salt.
2. Add in a skillet, large, then brown the beef on all sides. Drain.
3. Transfer the beef to a crockpot then add the onions.
4. Meanwhile, combine all the remaining ingredients in a mixing bowl and pour over the beef.
5. Cover the crockpot and cook for about 8-10 hours on low. Cook until tender then skim fat.
6. Thicken cooking liquid if desired.
7. Serve.

Nutrition Facts Per Serving

Calories: 243, total fat: 12g, saturated fat: 9g, total carbs: 10g, net carbs: 9g, protein: 23g, sugars: 7g, fiber: 1g, sodium: 443mg, potassium: 802mg

Shredded Green Chili Beef

Prep time: 25 minutes, cook time: 7 hours; serves 12

Ingredients

4 tbsp brown sugar, packed and divided
1 tbsp paprika
3 pounds beef chuck roast, boneless
28 ounces green enchilada sauce

What you'll need from store cupboard

2 thinly sliced and halved sweet onions, large
1½ tbsp salt
1 tbsp cayenne pepper
1 tbsp chili powder
1 tbsp garlic powder
½ tbsp pepper
2 tbsp canola oil

Instructions

1. Place 3tbsp sugar and onions in a crockpot, 5-qt or 6-qt.
2. In the meantime, combine 1 tbsp sugar, paprika, salt, cayenne pepper, chili powder, garlic powder, and pepper in a mixing bowl.
3. Marinate the beef with the mixture.
4. Now heat the oil in a skillet, large, and brown the beef for about 1-2 minutes over high-medium heat on each side.
5. Transfer the beef to a crockpot and pour the sauce over.
6. Cover the crockpot and cook for about 7-9 hours on low until beef is tender.
7. Remove from the pot then shred using two forks.
8. Return to the pot to heat through.
9. Serve with potatoes if desired.

Nutrition Facts Per Serving

Calories: 278, total fat: 15g, saturated fat: 4g, total carbs: 14g, net carbs: 13g, Protein: 23g, sugars: 8g, Fiber: 1g, sodium: 658mg, potassium: 743mg

Pork Stew

Prep time: 15 minutes, cook time: 5 hours; serves 8

Ingredients

2 pound pork tenderloins, 2-inch pieces
2 carrots, ½-inch slices
2 coarsely chopped celery ribs
1 fresh thyme sprig
1 fresh rosemary sprig

What you'll need from store cupboard

½ tbsp pepper
1 tbsp salt
1 coarsely chopped onion, medium
2 tbsp tomato paste
3 cups beef broth
4 minced garlic cloves
⅓ Cup pitted and chopped plums, dried
2 bay leaves

Instructions

1. Splash pepper and salt on the pork and transfer to a crockpot.
2. Add carrots, onion, and celery.
3. Meanwhile, whisk tomato paste, and beef broth in a bowl then pour over the vegetables.
4. Add garlic, plums, bay leaves, thyme, and rosemary.
5. Cover the crockpot and cook for about 5-6 hours on low until vegetables and pork are tender.
6. Discard thyme, bay leaves, and rosemary.
7. Serve with potatoes. Enjoy!

Nutrition Facts Per Serving

Calories: 177, total fat: 4g, saturated fat: 1g, total carbs: 9g, Net carbs: 8g, Protein: 24g, sugars: 4g, Fiber: 1g, sodium: 64mg, potassium: 99mg

Mexican Meatloaf

Prep time: 25 minutes, cook time: 4 hours; serves 8

Ingredients

2 tbsp Worcestershire sauce
12 crushed saltines
⅛ tbsp cayenne pepper
2 pounds lean beef, ground

What you'll need from store cupboard

6 tbsp divided ketchup
1 tbsp paprika
6 minced garlic cloves
½ tbsp pepper
½ tbsp salt

Instructions

1. Cut three heavy-duty foil into 20x3-inch, then crisscross to resemble wheel spokes. Place them in a crockpot, 3-qt, on the sides and the bottom. Use cooking spray to coat the strips.
2. Combine sauce, 2 tbsp ketchup, onion, saltines, paprika, garlic, pepper, salt, and cayenne in a bowl, large.
3. Now break the beef and mix well over the mixture.
4. Shape the mixture into a round loaf then place on the strips at the center.
5. Cover the crockpot and cook for about 4-5 hours on low until no pink is seen.
6. Transfer the meatloaf to a platter. Use the strips as handles.
7. Sprinkle the remaining ketchup over the meatloaf.
8. Serve and enjoy.

Nutrition Facts Per Serving

Calories: 222, total fat: 10g, saturated fat: 4g, total carbs: 10g, net carbs: 9g, protein: 23g, sugars: 5g, fiber: 1g, sodium: 447mg, potassium: 235mg

Chipotle Steak Simmer

Prep time: 15 minutes, cook time: 2 hours; serves 6

Ingredients

1½ lb top round roast, cubed
½ tbsp Mexican seasoning, salt-free
½ tbsp Adobo sauce, from the chipotle pepper can

1 tbsp Worcestershire sauce
2 cups canned tomatoes, crushed

What you'll need from store cupboard

¼ tbsp kosher salt
2 finely chopped chipotle peppers, from the can
1 tbsp brown sugar

3 tbsp olive oil
1½ cup red onion, 1-inch squares
1 tbsp finely minced garlic
1½ cup poblano pepper, 1-inch squares

Instructions

1. Place the roast into a bowl then season with salt and the seasoning. Mix to evenly coat and set aside.
2. Place finely chopped chipotle peppers to a bowl then add ½ tbsp adobo sauce, Worcestershire sauce, crushed tomatoes, and brown sugar. Mix to combine and set aside.
3. Add 1 tbsp olive to a hot nonstick skillet over medium heat. Add onion, garlic, and poblano peppers then spread to an even layer. Cook while occasionally stirring until crisp-tender and cooked evenly.
4. Transfer to a crockpot and return pan to heat.
5. Add 1 tbsp oil to the pan distributing evenly over the pan, then add half of seasoned roast cubes. Cook for about 1 minute on each side until browned.
6. Add the roast to the pot then stir in adobo and tomato mixture. Make sure the roast is submerged.
7. Cover the pot and cook for about 2-4 hours on low until the roast pulls apart easily with a fork.
8. Serve immediately and enjoy it.

Nutrition Facts Per Serving

Calories: 190, total fat: 6g, saturated fat: 2g, total carbs: 13g, net carbs: 11g, Protein: 26g, sugars: 7g, Fiber: 2g, sodium: 390mg, potassium: 570mg

Flank Steak Tacos

Prep time: 10 minutes, cook time: 6 hours; serves 12

Ingredients

1¼ lb flank steak
1 juiced lime
¾ cup Pico de Gallo
12, 6-inch corn tortillas

What you'll need from store cupboard

1 tbsp garlic powder
2 tbsp chili powder
1 tbsp cumin
½ cup water

Instructions

1. Place the steak in a crockpot then splash with garlic powder, chili powder, and cumin.
2. Pour lime juice over the steak then water.
3. Cover the crockpot and cook for about 6 hours on low until done.
4. Shred using a fork then scoop 1½ ounces to each tortilla.
5. Top 1 tbsp Pico de Gallo to each taco.
6. Enjoy.

Nutrition Facts Per Serving

Calories: 130, total fat: 4g, saturated fat: 1.5g, total carbs: 13g, net carbs: 11g, protein: 11g, sugars: 1g, fiber: 2g, sodium: 110mg, potassium: 240mg

Pork and Pumpkin Stew

Prep time: 15 minutes, cook time: 4 hours; serves 8

Ingredients
16 oz fat trimmed pork shoulder, 1-inch cubes
1/ tbsp salt-free seasoning
1 cup low-sodium beef broth
1 peeled and seeded pie pumpkin
4 fresh thyme sprigs

What you'll need from store cupboard
1 tbsp olive oil
2 tbsp tomato paste
¼ tbsp ground cinnamon
½ tbsp black pepper
1 large peeled onion
4 large diced celery stalks
3 large peeled carrots
4 minced garlic cloves
1 bay leaf
14 ounces rinsed and drained black beans

Instructions
1. Season the pork shoulder with seasoning and salt.
2. Add oil in a sauté pan and cook the seasoned pork for about 8 minutes until browned. Remove and set aside.
3. To the pan, add beef broth, tomato paste, and cinnamon, then whisk. This is to incorporate all brown bits on the pan bottom. Remove from heat.
4. Add liquid, browned pork and the remaining ingredients in a crockpot. Stir them to combine.
5. Cover and cook for about 3 hours 40 minutes on high.
6. Add beans, stir and cook for an additional 20 minutes. Remove bay leaf.
7. Serve and enjoy.

Nutrition Facts Per Serving
Calories: 150, total fat: 4g, saturated fat: 1g, total carbs: 15g, net carbs: 10g, protein: 14g, sugars: 4g, fiber: 5g, sodium: 170mg, potassium: 640mg

Chapter 9 Soups Stews And Curries

Rutabaga Stew

Prep time: 20 minutes, Cook time: 4 hours 5minutes; serves 15

Ingredients
24-ounce chicken, diced
4 rutabagas, peeled and diced
4 beets peeled and diced
4 carrots, diced
3 stalks celery, diced

What you'll need from the store cupboard
Cooking oil
1 red onion diced

Instructions
1. Heat cooking oil in a crockpot.
2. Stir cook chicken in hot oil until brown, about five minutes.
3. Add beets, rutabagas, carrots, onions, and celery to the pot,
4. Add enough water to cover completely.
5. Turn to low and simmer for at least 4 hours, add water to keep vegetables submerged.
6. Serve and enjoy

Nutritional facts per serves
Calories 111, total fats 2.1g, saturated fat 0.0g, total carbs 12.9g, net carbs 9.0, protein10.7g, sugar 8g, fiber 3.9g, sodium 80mg, potassium 560mg.

Coconut Shrimp Curry Recipe

Prep time: 5min, cook time: 2 hours; serves 6

Ingredients

1 lb cooked shrimp
1 cup chicken broth
1 tbsp ground ginger
1 bunch lemongrass
1 tbsp cilantro

What you'll need from the store cupboard

14 oz coconut milk
¼ Cup lemon juice

Instructions

1. Add all your ingredients in your crockpot.
2. Cook on high for two hours.
3. Eat as it is, or serve with spaghetti squash.

Nutritional Information per serving

Calories 293, total fats 17.9g, saturated fats 14.9, total carbs 15.1g, net carbs 13.5g, protein 20.4g, sugar 2.6g, fiber 1.6g, sodium 326mg, potassium 631mg.

Split Pea Soup

Prep time: 15 minutes, Cook time: 2 hours; serves 10

Ingredients
16 oz dried split peas
1 stalk celery, diced
2 large carrots, peeled and diced
2 cans low-fat chicken broth

What you'll need from the store cupboard
Salt and pepper to taste

Instructions
1. Rinse the peas and pick them through.
2. Place the peas in a crockpot together with celery, carrots chicken broth and water to boil.
3. Then reduce heat, simmer until peas have fallen apart, about 1 to 2 hours
4. Add salt and pepper to taste before serving.

Nutritional facts per serving
Calories 65, total fats 0.3g, saturated fats 0.0g, total carbs 11.2g, net carbs 6.6g, protein 4.8g, sugar 2g, fiber 4.6g, sodium 144mg, potassium 274mg.

Easter Ham Bone Soup

Prep time: 20min, Cook time: 1 hour 55 minutes; Serves 10

Ingredients

1 ham bone
5 potatoes
4 cups chopped cabbage
2 large stalks celery, chopped
1 cup light whipping cream

What you'll need from the store cupboard

12 cups water
⅓ Cup of all-purpose flour

Instructions

1. Put 12 cups of water and a ham bone in a crockpot and let boil until the meat comes off easily. Remove ham bone from the broth and let it cool to touch; remove meat from the bone and put in a resealable bag. Refrigerate.
2. Add broth into a mixing bowl, and refrigerate overnight. Skim any fat on top of the chilled broth and discard before transferring the broth to a large pot.
3. Bring it to boil, then add potatoes, celery, cabbage, and reserved ham, cook gently until potatoes are tender. This should take about 45 minutes.
4. Mix flour and half cup of water in a mixing bowl; blend into the potato-ham soup until consistent, add light cream and stir.
5. Serve and enjoy.

Nutritional facts Per Serving

Calories 111, Total fats 0.2g, Saturated fat 0.0g, Total carbs 24.8g, Net carbs 21.1, Protein 3.3g, Sugar 2g, Fiber 3.7g, Sodium 33mg, Potassium 570mg.

Pork And Green Chile Stew

Prep time: 25 minutes, Cook time: 4 hours 25 minutes; serves 6

Ingredients

2 pounds boneless sirloin pork roast or shoulder roast

15 ounces can hominy or whole -kernel corn drained

2tbsp quick-cooking tapioca

8 ounce diced green chile peppers

¼ tbsp dried oregano, crushed

What you will need from the store cupboard

1tbsp vegetable oil

½ cup chopped onion, medium size

4cups peeled and cubed tomatoes, medium size

3 cups water

1 tbsp garlic salt

½ tbsp ancho chile powder

½ tbsp ground cumin and pepper

¼ tbsp dried oregano, crushed

Chopped fresh cilantro, optional

Instructions

1. Remove excess fat from meat and cut into ½ -inch pieces
2. Add oil in large skillet and heat over medium-high heat. Sauté the onions and add half of the meat Cook until browned.
3. Remove the meat from the skillet using a slotted spoon. Repeat the process with the remaining meat.
4. Drain off fat and transfer meat to crockpot.
5. While stirring add in tomatoes, water hominy, tapioca, green chile peppers, garlic salt, ancho chili powder, cumin, ground pepper, and oregano.
6. Cover and cook on high for 4 to 5 hours or low for 7 to 8 hours.
7. Embellish each serving with cilantro.

Nutritional facts Per Serving

Calories 180g, total fats 4g, saturated fats 1g, total carbs 23g, net carbs 20g, protein 15g, sugar 2g, fiber; 3g, sodium 251mg, potassium 782mg.

Beefed-Up Vegetable Stew

Prep time: 30min, Cook time 5hour 5 minutes; serves 6

Ingredients

1lb lean ground beef
16-ounce stew vegetables, frozen
14 ounce can diced tomato with garlic, basil, and oregano
1 cube beef broth, reduced-sodium
½ tbsp garlic powder

What you'll need from the store cupboard

1 cup of water
½ tbsp onion powder
¼ tbsp black pepper

Instructions

1. Spray a nonstick skillet with cooking spray over medium heat. Brown the beef and drain it.
2. Spray your crockpot with cooking spray then add beef, stew vegetables, tomatoes, water, beef broth, garlic powder, onion powder, and black pepper.
3. Stir until well combined and cover.
4. Cook on low for five hours.
5. When the time elapses, serve and enjoy.

Nutritional facts per serving

Calories 199, total fats 8.0g saturated fats 3.1g, total carbs 14g, net carbs 9.8g, protein 18g, sugar 2.2g, sodium 115mg, potassium 760mg.

Flemish Beef Stew

Prep time: 30min, Cook time 5hour 5 minutes; serves 8

Ingredients
2 lb beef, bottom round, and fat trimmed off
¾ lb. cremini mushroom, sliced
2 cups brown ale
1 ½ tbsp Dijon mustard
1 tbsp caraway seeds

What you'll need from the store cupboard

4 tbsp canola oil	1 onion, chopped
3 tbsp all-purpose flour	1 bay leaf
4 carrots, peeled and cut into inch pieces	¾ tbsp salt
1 garlic clove, minced	½ tbsp ground pepper, fresh

Instructions
1. Heat two tablespoons of canola oil in a nonstick skillet. Add half of the beef and cook until brown on all sides.
2. Transfer the beef to your crockpot. Repeat the process with the remaining oil and beef.
3. Add mushrooms to the skillet and stir cook until liquid comes out and evaporates.
4. Sprinkle flour and cook without disturbing for ten seconds. Stir cook for thirty more seconds.
5. Add the brown ale and bring to boil. Cook until thick and bubbling. Transfer the mixture to the crockpot.
6. Add carrots, garlic, onions, Dijon mustard, seeds, bay leaf, salt, and pepper to the crockpot.
7. Lid the crockpot and set time for eight hours. When time is done remove the bay leaf from crockpot and serve. Enjoy.

Nutritional facts per serving
Calories 301, total fats 10g saturated fats 3g, total carbs 17g, net carbs 14g, protein 31g, sugar 5g, sodium 361mg, potassium 647mg.

French Onion Soup

Prep time: 30 minutes, Cook time 8hour 10 minutes; serves 8

Ingredients
2 lb yellow onions, sliced
2 lb red onions, sliced
4 cups beef broth, low sodium

What you'll need from the store cupboard
2 tbsp butter, cut into 8 pieces
2 tbsp olive oil
8 sprigs thyme
4 garlic cloves, smashed
1 bay leaf
1 tbsp salt
¾ tbsp pepper, ground
½ cup cherry

Instructions
1. Scatter butter in your crockpot.
2. Add oil, thyme, smashed garlic, bay leaf, yellow and red onions.
3. Sprinkle salt and pepper to taste and lid the crockpot — set the timer for eight hours.
4. Meanwhile, bring beef broth and sherry to boil in a skillet.
5. Remove the bay leaf and thyme sprigs from the crockpot and add the beef broth mixture.
6. Cook for ten more minutes. serve and enjoy when hot

Nutritional facts per serving
Calories 271, total fats 12g saturated fats 5 g, total carbs 31g, net carbs 9.8g, protein 12g, sugar 9g, sodium 529mg, potassium 428mg.

Chapter 10 Snacks

Scotch Eggs

Prep time: 15 minutes, cook time: 2 hours 20 minutes; Serves 2

Ingredients

2 eggs
1 ½ oz turkey breakfast sausages, lean
⅓ Cup brown rice Krispies cereal, crushed

Instructions

1. Place the eggs in your crockpot and add water such that the eggs are covered.
2. Set the timer for two and a half hours on high setting.
3. When time is over, remove from crockpot and place the eggs in ice-cold water. Peel the eggs and set aside.
4. Preheat oven to 4000F.
5. Scoop the sausage from its packaging using a spoon to make two patties with the rice cereal on your cutting board.
6. Place each egg on each patty and use additional sausage to cover the egg.
7. Transfer the scotched egg to a prepared cookie sheet and bake for twenty minutes or until the sausage is browned.
8. Serve and enjoy.

Nutrition Facts Per Serving

Calories 259, Total Fat 16.8g, Saturated Fat 5.3g, Total Carbs 9.0g, Net Carbs 7g, Protein 17.2g, Sugar 1.7g, Fiber 3g, Sodium 399mg, Potassium 210 mg

No Peel Crockpot Hard-Boiled Eggs

Prep time: 5 minutes, cook time: 1 hour 30 minutes; Serves 8

Ingredients

8 eggs
Unsalted butter

Instructions

1. Add two cups of water in your crockpot.
2. Butter an oven-safe bowl that fits your crockpot. Break the eggs to the buttered bowl ensuring the yolks don't break.
3. Cover and cook for an hour and a half or until the eggs look hard-boiled.
4. Loosen the edges with a spatula then remove the safe bowl from the crockpot.
5. Turn the bowl on a cutting board and chop the eggs to your desired consistency.
6. Serve and enjoy the eggs with a salad of choice.

Nutrition Facts Per Serving

Calories 63, Total Fat 4g, Saturated Fat 1g, Total Carbs 1g, Net Carbs 0g, Protein 6g, Sugar 1g, Fiber 0.1g, Sodium 62 mg, Potassium 61 mg

Deviled Eggs

Prep time: 20 minutes, cook time: 1 hour 30 minutes; Serves 12

Ingredients

6 eggs
2 tbsp light mayonnaise
⅛ tbsp mustard powder
1 black pepper, freshly ground

What you'll need from the store cupboard

1 pinch salt
I scallion, sliced (for garnish)
Grape tomatoes (for garnish)

Instructions

1. Place the eggs in your crockpot and add water such that the eggs are covered.
2. Set the timer for two and a half hours on HIGH.
3. When time is over, remove from crockpot and place the eggs in ice-cold water. Peel the eggs cut them vertically.
4. Remove the yolks and place them in a mixing bowl. Add mayonnaise, mustard powder pepper, and salt, then mash using a folk.
5. Fill the egg whites with the mayo mixture and garnish with scallions and grape tomatoes.
6. Serve and enjoy.

Nutrition Facts Per Serving

Calories 45, Total Fat 3g, Saturated Fat 1g, Total Carbs 1g, Net Carbs 0g, Protein 3g, Sugar 0g, Fiber 0g, Sodium 70mg, Potassium 35 mg

Turkey Breasts

Prep time: 20 minutes, cook time: 6 hours; Serves 4

Ingredients

1 turkey breast
1 tbsp garlic powder
1 tbsp paprika
1 tbsp parsley

Instructions

1. Place the turkey breast in a crockpot.
2. Season with garlic, parsley, and paprika. Let sit to marinate for five minutes.
3. Set timer for six hours. When the time elapses, remove the turkey from the crockpot and place it on a cutting board.
4. Cover with aluminum foil and let rest for ten minutes.
5. Cut into pieces and serve. Enjoy.

Nutrition Facts Per Serving

Calories 140, Total Fat 3g, Saturated Fat 1g, Total Carbs 0g, Net Carbs 0g, Protein 27g, Sugar 0g, Fiber 0g, Sodium 41mg, Potassium 42 mg

Pumpkin Muffins

Prep time: 10 minutes, cook time: 45 minutes; Serves 5

Ingredients

½ cup pumpkin pieces
1 banana (ripe)
1 cup milk
½ tbsp pumpkin pie spice
2 tbsp raisins

What you'll need from the store cupboard

Cooking spray
1 tbsp brown sugar, granulated
¼ tbsp salt
1 egg yolk

Instructions

1. Add water and pumpkin pieces in your crockpot. Cook in high for one hour.
2. When time elapses, remove the pumpkin from the crockpot and let it rest.
3. Preheat your oven to 3000F and spray five standard muffin cups with cooking spray.
4. Add all the ingredients in a food processor except the raisins. Blend until very smooth.
5. Stir in the raisins, then scoop the mixture into the muffin cups, then bake for forty-five minutes.
6. Let the cake rest then unmold from them from the muffin cups.
7. Serve and enjoy.

Nutrition Facts Per Serving

Calories 75, Total Fat 2g, Saturated Fat 0.5g, Total Carbs 15g, Net Carbs 14g, Protein 2g, Sugar 3g, Fiber 1g, Sodium 133mg, Potassium 70 mg

Popcorns

Prep time: 30 minutes, cook time: 30 minutes; Serves 4

Ingredients

4 tbsp coconut oil
1 cup Safeway popcorn

What you'll need from the store cupboard

4 tbsp butter
¼ Himalayan salt

Instructions

1. Add coconut oil in your crockpot and swirl it so that the bottom is well covered. Heat the crockpot until the oil sizzles.
2. Add the popcorn and use a wooden spatula to coat them well with oil.
3. Cover with a clear lid so that you will see when most of the popcorn has popped.
4. Turn off the heat and remove the lid. Pour the popcorn into a bowl and let it rest for two minutes.
5. Add butter and salt to taste. Serve and enjoy.

Nutrition Facts Per Serving

Calories 186, Total Fat 13g, Saturated Fat 9g, Total Carbs 14g, Net Carbs 12g, Protein 2g, Sugar 3g, Fiber 2g, Sodium 124mg, Potassium 56 mg

Meatloaf on A Sling

Prep time: 30 minutes, cook time: 5 hours; Serves 4

Ingredients
⅓ Cup ketchup
2 tbsp Worcestershire sauce
1 lb. beef, ground
⅔ Cup oats, quick-cooking
2 tbsp flaxseed, ground

What you'll need from the store cupboard
Nonstick cooking spray
1 tbsp water
½ cup onion, chopped
¾ cup green bell pepper, diced
½ cup egg substitute
⅛ tbsp salt

Instructions
1. Spray the crockpot with cooking spray.
2. Add ketchup Worcestershire sauce and water in a mixing bowl and mix.
3. In a separate bowl, combine beef, oats, flaxseed, onions, bell pepper, egg substitute salt, and three tablespoons of the ketchup mixture. Store the remaining ketchup in a fridge.
4. Lengthwise, fold paper foil sheets into half. Coat the strips with cooking spray then crisscross them in spoke like way. They will act as a sling.
5. Now place the meatloaf mixture at the center of the spokes.
6. Transfer the leaf to the crockpot, ensuring the aluminum foil in place for easy removal.
7. Cover the crockpot and cook on low for five hours.
8. Evenly apply the remaining ketchup mixture on the meatloaf and let it rest for fifteen minutes.
9. Carefully lift the foil strips to remove the meatloaf from the crockpot.
10. Serve and enjoy.

Nutrition Facts Per Serving
Calories 259, Total Fat 7.7g, Saturated Fat 2.8g, Total Carbs 19g, Net Carbs 15g, Protein 32g, Sugar 6.5g, Fiber 3g, Sodium 409mg, Potassium 142 mg

Chipotle BBQ Pork Folded Tacos

Prep time: 30 minutes, cook time: 4 hours; Serves 4

Ingredients
2 garlic cloves
1 cup barbecue sauce, reduced sugar
4 chipotle chili peppers, purred
2 lb. pork shoulder, trimmed
16 whole-wheat tortillas, low carb

What you'll need from the store cupboard
1 ½ tbsp smoked paprika
1 ½ cup onions, diced
2 cups cabbage, shredded

Instructions
1. Combine garlic cloves, sauce, and chipotle peppers in a blender and blend well. Let rest in a refrigerator.
2. Place the pork in your crockpot and cook on high for four hours. Transfer the pork on your cutting board.
3. Use a fork to shred the pork discarding excess fat. Return the pot to your crockpot.
4. Sprinkle the smoked paprika and barbecue sauce mixture then cook on low for one hour. Skim off excess fat.
5. Warm the tortillas and place a heaping spoonful of cooked pork. Top with onions and cabbage.
6. Serve and enjoy.

Nutrition Facts Per Serving
Calories 160, Total Fat 7g, Saturated Fat 2g, Total Carbs 15g, Net Carbs 7g, Protein 15g, Sugar 3g, Fiber 8g, Sodium 350mg, Potassium 230 mg

Chapter 11 Desserts

Creme Brulee

Prep time: 20 minutes, cook time: 2 hours; Serves 4

Ingredients
4 egg yolks
¼ cup white sugar
1 ⅔ cups whipping cream, heavy
2 tbsp vanilla extract

What you'll need from the store cupboard
¼ tbsp salt

Instructions
1. In a mixing bowl, whisk together egg yolks, quarter cup sugar, and salt.
2. Whisk in whipping cream and vanilla extract. Strain the custard mixture into a measuring cup.
3. Line the crockpot bottom with folded kitchen towel. Place the ramekins on the towel and fill the crockpot with water such that the water comes halfway the ramekins.
4. Pour the custard mixture into ramekins then drape the towel over the crockpot. Place the lid the crockpot.
5. Set the timer for two hours so that the custard jiggles a little bit but is set.
6. Remove the ramekins from the crockpot and let them rest to completely cool.

Nutrition Facts Per Serving
Calories 255, Total Fat 41.1g, Saturated Fat 24g, Total Carbs 20g, Net Carbs 0g, Protein 4.7g, Sugar 4g, Fiber 0g, Sodium 191mg, Potassium 96mg

Cider Applesauce

Prep time: 20 minutes, cook time: 5 hours; Serves 16

Ingredients
5 lb. apples, peeled, cored and sliced
1 ½ tbsp cinnamon, ground
½ tbsp garlic cloves, ground

What you'll need from the store cupboard
¼ tbsp nutmeg, ground

Instructions
1. Layer the apples slices on your crockpot.
2. Sprinkle cinnamon, garlic, and nutmeg over the apple slices.
3. Lid the crockpot and cook for five hours. When time elapses, let the apple rest to cool.
4. Use an immersion blender to blend the apples until smooth.
5. Serve your applesauce and enjoy it.

Nutrition Facts Per Serving
Calories 76, Total Fat 0.3g, Saturated Fat 0.0g, Total Carbs 20.2g, Net Carbs 17g, Protein 0.4g, Sugar 15g, Fiber 3.8g, Sodium 2mg, Potassium 155mg

Crockpot Sugar-Free Chocolate Molten Lava Cake

Prep time: 10 minutes, cook time: 3 hours; Serves 12

Ingredients

1 ½ Cup swerve sweetener, divided
½ cup flour, gluten-free
5 tbsp cocoa powder, unsweetened and divided
4 oz chocolate chips, sugar-free

What you'll need from the store cupboard

½ tbsp salt
1 tbsp baking powder
½ cup butter, melted and cooled
3 eggs
3 egg yolks
½ tbsp vanilla liquid stevia
1 tbsp vanilla extract
2 cups hot water

Instructions

1. Grease your crockpot with cooking spray.
2. Whisk together one and a half cup swerve sweetener, flour, three tablespoon cocoa, baking powder, and salt.
3. In another mixing bowl, mix butter, eggs, egg yolks, liquid stevia, and vanilla extract.
4. Add the wet mixture to the dry mixture and mix until well combined.
5. Pour the mixture to the crockpot and top with chocolate chips.
6. Whisk together the remaining swerve sweetener and cocoa powder. Pour over the chocolate chips in the crockpot.
7. Lid the crockpot and set time for three hours. When time is done, let sit to cool.
8. Serve and enjoy.

Nutrition Facts Per Serving

Calories 157, Total Fat 13g, Saturated Fat 6.4g, Total Carbs 10.5g, Net Carbs 7.9g, Protein 3.9g, Sugar 0.2g, Fiber 2.6g, Sodium 166mg, Potassium 106mg

Maple Custard

Prep time: 20 minutes, cook time: 2 hours; Serves 6

Ingredients

1 cup heavy cream, organic
½ cup whole milk, organic
¼ cup sukrin Gold
½ tbsp cinnamon

What you'll need from the store cupboard

2 egg yolks
2 eggs
1 tbsp maple extract
1 tbsp salt

Instructions

1. Combine all ingredients in a blender and blend until well combined.
2. Grease ramekins with butter then pour the mixture into each ramekin up to three-quarters full.
3. Place four ramekins at the bottom of the crockpot and the remaining two on top of the bottom ramekins but against the crockpot sides.
4. Place the lid and set the timer for two hours on high. When time elapses, remove the ramekins from the crockpot.
5. Let rest for one hour to cool. Sprinkle more cinnamon then serve and enjoy.

Nutrition Facts Per Serving

Calories 190, Total Fat 18g, Saturated Fat 10g, Total Carbs 2g, Net Carbs 0g, Protein 4g, Sugar 1g, Fiber 0g, Sodium 144mg, Potassium 83mg

Fudge Cake

Prep time: 5 minutes, cook time: 1hours 30 minutes; Serves 8

Ingredients

15 ¼ oz Betty Crocker Chocolate Fudge Cake
4 oz Jell-O Chocolate Instant pudding mix
⅔ Cup sour cream
11 ½ oz Smuckers Hot Fudge Sauce

What you'll need from the store cupboard

4 eggs
¾ Cup Vegetable Oil

Instructions

1. Combine all ingredients in a mixing bowl and let sit for two minutes.
2. Spray your crockpot with cooking spray then transfer the mixture to the crockpot.
3. Cover the crockpot and set the timer for one and a half hours. When time elapses, transfer the cake to serving bowls and drizzle with hot fudge sauce.

Nutrition Facts Per Serving

Calories 150, Total Fat 4.1g, Saturated Fat 2.2g, Total Carbs 26.9g, Net Carbs 22.1g, Protein 5.4g, Sugar 14g, Fiber 3.3g, Sodium 154mg, Potassium 0mg

Key Lime Dump Cake

Prep time: 5 minutes, cook time: 2 hours; Serves 4

Ingredients
44 oz Key lime filling
15 ¼ oz Betty Crocker Vanilla Cake mix

What you'll need from the store cupboard
Cooking spray
8 tbsp butter, melted

Instructions
1. Spray the crockpot with cooking spray then spread the lime filling at the bottom.
2. Combine the cake mix and butter in a mixing bowl.
3. Pour the mixture over lime filling and spread it evenly.
4. Cover the crockpot with the lid and set time for two hours.
5. When time elapses, serve and enjoy with whip cream.

Nutrition Facts Per Serving
Calories 197, Total Fat 23g, Saturated Fat 4g, Total Carbs 18g, Net Carbs 16g, Protein 3.4g, Sugar 23g, Fiber 0.3g, Sodium 296mg, Potassium 63mg

Peppermint Chocolate Pudding Cake

Prep time: 10 minutes, cook time: 3 hours; Serves 4

Ingredients

15 ¼ Chocolate cake mix
¼ tbsp peppermint extract
3 cups milk, low fat
3 ½ oz chocolate cook and serve pudding and pie filling mix, sugar-free and fat-free

What you'll need from the store cupboard

1 cup water
⅓ Cup canola oil
3 eggs, refrigerated and light beaten

Instructions

1. Coat your crockpot liner with cooking spray and set aside.
2. In a mixing bowl, combine cake mix, peppermint extract, water, oil, and eggs. Pour the mixture in the prepared crockpot.
3. In another bowl, whisk together milk and pudding. Pour in a saucepan and heat until it just simmers. Remove from heat.
4. Pour the pudding mixture over the cake mix mixture. Lid the crockpot and set time for three hours.
5. Remove the liner from the crockpot and let the cake rest to cool. Serve and enjoy.

Nutrition Facts Per Serving

Calories 185, Total Fat 7g, Saturated Fat 2g, Total Carbs 27g, Net Carbs 22g, Protein 4g, Sugar 14g, Fiber 1g, Sodium 233mg, Potassium 181mg

Printed in Great Britain
by Amazon